P9-DOG-838

TWENTIETH CENTURY INTERPRETATIONS OF

ENDGAME

TWENTIETH CENTURY INTERPRETATIONS OF ENDGAME

A Collection of Critical Essays

Edited by

BELL GALE CHEVIGNY

Prentice-Hall, Inc. 

Englewood Cliffs, N. J.

Quotations from *Endgame followed by Act without Words* (New York: Grove Press, Inc., 1958; London: Faber & Faber Ltd. Copyright © 1958 by Grove Press, Inc.) used by permission of the publishers.

C–13-277293-0; P–13-277285-x. *Library of Congress Catalog Card Number 78-90967.* Printed in the United States of America.

Current printing (last number):
10 9 8 7 6 5 4 3 2 1

PRENTICE-HALL INTERNATIONAL (*London*)
PRENTICE-HALL OF AUSTRALIA, PTY. LTD. (*Sydney*)
PRENTICE-HALL OF CANADA, LTD. (*Toronto*)
PRENTICE-HALL OF INDIA PRIVATE LIMITED (*New Delhi*)
PRENTICE-HALL OF JAPAN, INC. (*Tokyo*)

Contents

Introduction

by Bell Gale Chevigny

The narrator of Beckett's story "The Calmative" loses his way and asks directions of a man who, in turn, demands of him the story of his life: "No details, he said, the main drift, the main drift." [1] This could stand as motto not only for Beckett's creative policy, but also for his life, at least so far as it is known. Remarkably little detail about him is available, but the drift is plain—a drift like that of so many Irish writers, and especially his early mentor, James Joyce, away from the restrictions of Ireland to the privacy and creative freedom of Europe. Born near Dublin in 1906, the son of a Protestant quantity surveyor, Beckett distinguished himself at Trinity College in French and Italian and was sent in 1928 as exchange lecturer to the Ecole Normale Supérieure in Paris, where he came to know Joyce. Back at Trinity in 1930, he earned a master's degree for research on Descartes and taught French, but only for four terms, after which he quit abruptly and wandered aimlessly in Europe until 1937 when he settled in Paris. Returning to Ireland only to visit his family, he was there when war broke out in 1939, hurrying him back to France. "I preferred France in war to Ireland in peace," he has said,[2] and he worked with a Resistance group in Paris until it was discovered in 1942; then he fled to Vaucluse in the Unoccupied Zone to work as a farm laborer. After the war in Europe he worked briefly in St. Lô with the Irish Red Cross before returning to Paris and concentrated writing. Now he divides his time between the city and a country cottage bought with royalties from *Waiting for Godot*. A biographical sketch by Rayner Heppenstall captures Beckett's tone: "As to his own domestic circumstances, Mr. Beckett seems a little in doubt whether he should be described as a married man, but is certain there are no children." [3] Beckett's

[1] *Stories and Texts for Nothing* (New York: Grove Press, Inc., 1967), p. 40. Unless otherwise indicated, all subsequent Beckett citations are from Grove Press editions of his work.

[2] Israel Shenker, "Moody Man of Letters," *New York Times*, May 6, 1956, sec. 2, p. 1.

[3] Rayner Heppenstall, *The Fourfold Tradition* (London: Barrie and Rockliff, 1961), p. 258.

chariness with detail, even in a joke about himself, is tied to his skepticism; in literature he seeks ever to raise the threshold of certainty.

Beckett's work too traces a progress in alienation and freedom, a clearing away of excrescences to make a placeless place where increasingly primal uncertainties may be known. He was first attracted to the linguistic emancipation of his friend Joyce, and in Paris in his early twenties he began a French translation of part of the developing *Finnegan's Wake* and wrote a brilliant explication. Shortly afterwards he wrote a commissioned monograph on Proust, celebrating that master's escape from time, and at the same time his first poem, *Whoroscope,* supplemented, in imitation of Eliot, with explanatory footnotes. In subsequent stories (*More Pricks than Kicks*), poems (*Echo's Bones*), and in his first two novels (*Murphy* and *Watt*), Beckett gradually exorcised his linguistic flamboyance. When, after the war, he ensconced himself in his Paris room to write for about five years, he was working literally in the limited and solipsistic setting that is the spiritual landscape for all his major work. He wrote almost everything that made him known at this time (*Molloy, Malone Dies, The Unnamable, Waiting for Godot,* and *Stories and Texts for Nothing*), and he deepened his exile by writing them all in French. Adopting French was another means of paring away, replacing the resonant suggestiveness of English with an idiom more precise and abstract, although later he tried to preserve his gains by translating these works into English.

After the trilogy of novels and the *Texts for Nothing,* Beckett thought he had reached a creative impasse. As he told Israel Shenker, "For some authors writing gets easier the more they write. For me it gets more and more difficult. For me the area of possibilities gets smaller and smaller." [4] But frustration is also promise in Beckett's peculiar art. In "Three Dialogues," debates with Georges Duthuit which are perhaps imaginary, Beckett disparages art composed on the field of the possible: "I speak of an art turning from it in disgust, weary of its puny exploits, weary of pretending to be able, of being able, of doing a little better the same old thing, of going a little further along a dreary road." He prefers a consciously impossible art, "the expression that there is nothing to express, nothing with which to express, nothing from which to express, no power to express, no desire to express, together with the obligation to express." [5]

[4] Shenker, *New York Times,* p. 3.

[5] *Samuel Beckett: A Collection of Critical Essays* (Englewood Cliffs, N.J.: Prentice-Hall, Inc., 1965), p. 17. Reprinted from *Transition forty-nine,* No. 5 (1949).

So, after producing nothing new for six years, in 1956 Beckett completed *Fin de Partie,* which was at once a way out of the impasse and an expression of it and more than *Godot* a dramatization of the thwarted and unchartable findings of the fiction. Translating it into English as *Endgame* perhaps induced him to write first in English, then in French his next plays (*Krapp's Last Tape, Happy Days,* and *Play*), which are briefer explorations of the same terrain. And more recently there have been modulations in other media, translations of Beckett's world for other senses—plays and playlets for radio and television, a film, gnomic fictions and the strange verse-novel *Comment C'est* (*How it is*).

Endgame may be regarded as part of a general enterprise to find the main drift of life by going to life's perimeters. Peggy Guggenheim, who met Beckett in 1937, calls attention to his style of marginal living by naming him Oblomov, after the hero of Goncharov's novel who couldn't get out of bed. More suggestively, she recalls that he was haunted by a literally marginal memory, a prenatal one: "Ever since his birth he had retained a terrible memory of life in his mother's womb. He was constantly suffering from this and had awful crises, when he felt he was suffocating." [6] It is interesting that this situation is evoked by the womb-like room of the play and by Hamm's condition even while he is waiting for the end of life. As Jerry Tallmer projected the vision of the play in his review of the Cherry Lane production: "Imagine a foetus, doomed to be stillborn, suspended in darkness in the amniotic fluid, its life-not-to-be leaking away through the fontanelle—the membraneous gap at the top of the skull of every human embryo." [7] Tallmer here alludes to Hamm's line, "Something dripping in my head, ever since the fontanelles," which ties the feminine womb image to the other major image suggested by the play's setting—the masculine image of the room as a skull with two windows as sightless eyes.

Womb and skull—the conscious and unconscious waiting-rooms to living itself—point to a third image for *Endgame*'s setting. One of Beckett's oldest and most persistent "places" is the Ante-Purgatory where men who procrastinated in repenting were doomed to wait out their life-span again before being admitted to the cleansing pain of Purgatory. Here Dante found Belacqua, as in a womb and in a skull, crouching in the foetal posture, dreaming over again his life which even in Florence had been one of dreaming. In Florence he had been

[6] *Out of this Century* (New York: The Dial Press, 1946), p. 205.

[7] *The Village Voice,* Feb. 5, 1958, p. 7.

fond of quoting to Dante the Aristotelian dictum, *"sedendo et quiescendo anima efficitur sapiens"* (by sitting and remaining quiet the mind is made wise), and now in the nether world he asked him, "Brother, what avails it to ascend?" Beckett named his earliest burlesque hero, in the Joycean *More Pricks than Kicks,* Belacqua Shuah, and, as his work progressed, deepened his appreciation of the original's procrastination and regressive dream. And Ante-Purgatory came to seem increasingly a precise metaphor for the kind of space and time that inspired Beckett, between void and being, when life is over though neither finished nor begun—very much the date and address of *Endgame.* Belacqua is variously present in the bitter lyrical reminiscence of an earlier life by Nell and Nagg, and, in Clov's final hovering on the threshold, more likely to relive the day-cycle than to move into another phase. Hamm, whose posture is a grim *sedendo,* an enforced refusal to ascend, replies to Clov's question, "Do you believe in the life to come?" by saying mordantly, "Mine was always that." This, the darkest of Beckett's versions of Belacqua, suggests a man who dreams obliquely forward as well as backward. The play's intense inaction then seems a response to an awareness of purgatory-to-come in lieu of active purgation—the condition of a Hamm who contemplates a future with no more pain-killer.

Womb, skull, and lifelong vigil combine to lead us deep into Beckett's imaginative universe and to prepare us for its curious drama. Here consciousness, the solipsistic action of the skull, is a travesty of the timeless and self-possessed life in the womb, and a bitter reminder of loss. Beckett's characters live for an end to the exile of consciousness, knowing they are like one of the speakers in *Texts for Nothing,*

> beyond all doubt on earth, for as long as it takes to die again, wake again, long enough for things to change here, for something to change, to make possible a deeper birth, a deeper death, or resurrection in and out of this murmur of memory and dream.

The deep change they await is simultaneously a death of divisive consciousness and a birth into whole selfhood, even if selfhood should be the experience of nothingness. But the prospective change to being and the void is remote, and it fades. "The end is in the beginning and yet you go on": this is Hamm's merciless knowledge, and he waits, he goes on, cursed and blessed by consciousness which prolongs the wait even as it relieves it. This is clearer in *Endgame* than in *Godot* where the characters looked for resolution from without—from Godot, from the wings, from their own faith which, however enfeebled, necessarily bears reference to something outer. In *Endgame* all outside is Zero, man cannot help his fellow man even to his death, consciousness lacks external reference; one looks inward, like Hamm thrice blinded, to find an impossible end, a cessation of that endless self-consciousness which is never self-possession.

The phenomenon of the elusive or divided self is developed as the crucial metaphysical, psychological, and aesthetic problem by Beckett. Like the phenomenologists and existentialists, especially Husserl and Sartre, to whose fundamental inquiries Beckett's own are kin, Beckett is haunted by Descartes and can never be done with his celebrated starting-point. He seeks throughout his work to accept the finality of the Cartesian *cogito ergo sum* by endless cogitation, but ironically only thus recedes from the "I am." In modern literature Beckett's clearest antecedent is Dostoevsky's *Notes from Underground* in which the speaker is shown first superior to his fellows in self-consciousness, then inferior in action, the bodying forth of consciousness; although he yearns for a perfect freedom of self-possession, he is caught in the contradictory babble of the disowned ego. In his adopted culture, Beckett is the ironic heir of Rimbaud. *"Je est un autre"*—the poet's romantic and euphoric formula of self-alienation, meant to be the source of song and the liberation of the ego, is now so inhibiting that neither song nor ego can be identified. Each of Beckett's characters hears in his own voice a foreign accent (we may read this as another "explanation" for Beckett's use of French—the language itself standing for his ontological exile). Each speaks with a voice that can neither stop nor satisfy the speaker. Whose is this voice? In *Molloy* it is an authority variously called "prompter," "imperative," and "employer." It exacts of Molloy and Moran not only their mysterious forced marches but also detailed reports, and yet at the novel's end it becomes clear that both voyage and tale may be fiction:

> I have spoken of a voice telling me things. . . . It told me to write the report. Does that mean that I am freer now than I was? I do not know. I shall learn. Then I went back into my house and wrote, It is midnight. The rain is beating on the windows. It was not midnight. It was not raining.

Here the authority is finally the ambiguous creative impulse, which unites utter subservience and the freedom of complete invention. Issuing "hypothetical imperatives" as Molloy wittily terms them, the voice reveals the writer as both master and servant. But in *Malone Dies* it is hinted that by the circuitous route of invention one hunts the real self. Making up stories on his deathbed, Malone pauses to ask, "I wonder if I am not talking yet again about myself. Shall I be incapable, to the end, of lying on any other subject?" *The Unnamable* is the most sustained agony over the voice in the work of relating it to whatever might be understood as "I": "let me hasten to take advantage of being now obliged to say, in a manner of speaking, there is I, on the one hand, and this noise on the other." Until the gap is healed, the voice is without self as well as body, and man talking is a performer. The image of the actor is underscored in *Texts for Nothing*: "who's this speaking in me, and who's this disowning me, as though I had taken his place, usurped his life," and "here I'm a mere ventriloquist's dummy." Finally the two opening lines of the verse-novel *How it is* include the phrases, "I quote," and "I say it as I hear it," which are then interpolated throughout the text, like parodic footnotes.

How is a play made from this trouble? Some critics have felt Beckett's vision of the self's disintegration more suited to fiction than to the stage where concrete things and solid bodies indisputably exist. We must disagree for several reasons. First, his primary image of disintegration, as we have seen, is a voice perhaps of the self, but conceivably of a devil, invader, boss, or author *who prompts from without*—this is an inherently theatrical conceit. (Indeed Beckett employs the ambiguity of voice literally in both his television play *Eh Joe,* where we see only Joe and hear only the voice of the woman speaking in his mind, continually redefining him before our eyes, and in *Krapp's Last Tape,* a subtle exploration of the gap between the "I" of the present and the noise of the past as recorded on the tape.)

Then too, since the stage speaker, unlike the speakers in the late fiction, has not only the reader (or audience) for auditor, but other stage speakers as well, speaking has more resonance. The odds mount both for and against self-discovery. Beckett discerns in his drama that unrelatedness to others is the simplest of metaphors for unrelatedness to self. In the heavy pauses between speeches the audience is made to experience the gaping distances in the characters. Or the dialogue itself, a travesty of communication, reflects this, most plainly in Nagg's and Nell's heartbreakingly funny struggle to talk ("Our hearing hasn't failed." "Our what?"). We are reminded of Beckett's discussion of friendship in his essay on Proust: "the attempt to communicate where no communication is possible is merely a simian vulgarity, like the madness that holds a conversation with the furniture." Hamm and Clov sometimes represent the poles of the self's unrelatedness—Hamm as the prompter, Clov as the speech. Clov seems often to be only a figment of the imagination of others. "I use the words you taught me," he says, and asked for a few words from his "heart," he begins, "they said to me." But near the end Clov appears to know that the only freedom he can gain from master, father, creator is self-possession, for which the threatened departure is only the outward and futile show: "I say to myself—sometimes, Clov, you must be there better than that if you want them to let you go—one day."

For all his bulk and force, Hamm is continually slipping away before our eyes. By bullying Clov, writing his responses, Hamm tries to equate power with the conviction that he exists. Trying to equate being perceived with being, he also bribes Nagg to listen and in bitter self-mockery props up a toy dog. His chronicle is an attempt to wrest his own confession from his fiction. He labors over variations, in the spirit of one of the voices in *Texts for Nothing* who, without wholly crediting it, asserts in countless ways that he is there: "That's why I say it, patiently, variously, trying to vary, for you never know, it's perhaps all a question of hitting on the right aggregate." Should the formula be hit, his brute physical presence and his voice would coincide at last with real presence (or the felt absence with physical absence), the doors of Purgatory would open, and the strange anguish be done. (*Comédie,* the French version of *Play,* ingeniously takes its form from this nostalgia for the right aggregate. Oblivious of each other, three characters tell fragments of their stories and the play ends by directing a reprise in which the sequence of speeches may be varied.) But Beckett never allows us to believe that either resolution will come about. Although Hamm behaves as though he might arrive at a credible self through self-imitation or discover consistent being through dogged repetition or find through acting out a route out of acting, he knows the ruse lurking in all roles from the play's beginning when he says, "The bigger a man is the fuller he is. And the emptier." So it is with Hamm, whose most vivid presence co-exists with a radical expression of absence which infects the play and is finally declared in Hamm's admission, "I was never there."

Beckett's obsessions with the illusion of life and the elusiveness of being, made brilliantly dramatic in *Endgame,* are historically tied to the conditions of theatre at their most profound. As spectators we identify with a character on the stage more than in other arts, but we always know him for an actor who reads an invisible script. Thus our belief and our skepticism are deeply engaged at once—a condition which is shared by Beckett the author and his creatures. Something like this double response is as old as Greek drama, which built suspense in the hearts of spectators who knew the story by heart. Closer still is Shakespeare, whose Hamlet generates vibrating circles of meaning, bringing us spectators on the stage as actors to watch him watch Claudius and Gertrude watch the players who read a patently artificial script as surely (but less patently) as do Gertrude and Claudius and Hamlet and we. Hamm's line, "Imagine if a rational being came back to earth, wouldn't he be liable to get ideas into his head if he observed us long enough," is an echo of this tradition in Shakespeare.

But Beckett is closer still to a tradition of modern theatre which explores further this craft-conscious strain in Shakespeare and ties it to the post-romantic preoccupation with subjectivity and solipsism. Pirandello was the first to treat as the overt and primary content of stage drama the problematic nature of artistic form, the built-in inadequacy of communication, and the multiplicity of personality. Beckett pursues these same concerns in his plays, but with the huge difference in feeling from Pirandello that exists between one who thinks a problem conquered when declared and one who knows its implacability. For Pirandello, the display of the dramatists difficulty itself constituted a new "fecundating matrix" for art, which realistic drama had lost. Beckett is as far from celebrating the problem as he is from crying with Nagg's tailor: "look—at the world—and look—at my TROUSERS!"

Beckett superficially resembles Ionesco when the latter's plays attack the very form he uses, progress from conventional satire to a satire without an informing norm, produce a "hero in spite of himself" (as Ionesco once described him[8]), a man of unreason beyond social recall, and culminate in the breakdown of communication. But Beckett begins with premises which Ionesco only adumbrates at the end. The very fact that Ionesco's plays develop and then demolish conventions is a concession to those conventions and to the audience that needs to be educated beyond them. Thus, where Beckett is monochromatic, Ionesco depends on contrast. His unreasoning hero is presented with a reasoning foil, his isolation is set in relief by recognizable social types. The failure of communication is thus different in kind. For Ionesco, whose characters represent real alternatives in a still familiar world, it is the breakdown of social communication; for Beckett, whose characters are more like interdependent aspects of one another, one another's voice or eye in an absent world, it is the breakdown of communication with one's self.

If Beckett's rigor continually reveals that the art of Pirandello and Ionesco cuts through conventional illusion only to institute smugly a new illusion, so does Genet's. The integrity of both Beckett and Genet comes from their unrelenting vigilance over illusion. Their

[8] Rosette C. Lamont, "The Hero in Spite of Himself," *Yale French Studies,* No. 29 (Spring-Summer, 1962), 73–81.

characters share the skepticism of the authors and strikingly anticipate that of the audience by continually undercutting whatever might have been convincing, belying what seemed authentic, exploding all behavior as self-conscious performance. Genet and Beckett further recognize that even this creates a problem, because by stripping away illusion they are in danger of seeming to arrive at truth. Their consequent strategy is to deny apparent truth and achievement by calling them further illusion. As artists, they are caught forever in the absurd posture not only of erasing what they have done, but repudiating even the act of erasure. This is reflected in the circular structure of their plays. *The Blacks* ends with the cast dancing the minuet from *Don Giovanni* as they did when the play began, as *Happy Days* ends with Winnie replaying the "Merry Widow" waltz on her music box as she did in Act I: in both cases change is cancelled by the circle. (All of Beckett's plays suggest the reprise literally prescribed at the end of *Comédie*. *Godot* points to a third similar day, Krapp's tape revolves forever, and *Endgame*'s end may only be a game, to be resumed tomorrow, "the same as usual.")

Despite the shared merciless aesthetic integrity, the effects gained by the two playwrights could scarcely differ more: Genet's stage is usually a hive of business, a kaleidoscope of costume, where Beckett's is static and gray. It is as if they divided the emphasis of their common premise: we are unable to grasp Being; appearance is in our hand. In despair of Being, Genet designs a dance with the many veils of appearance; endlessly stripping away appearances, Beckett keeps confronting the despair of Being. Notwithstanding the built-in disclaimers, Genet's work surges with energy and life, which in Beckett are always deliberately fading.

This comparison suggests Beckett's own comparison of himself with Joyce:

> the difference is that Joyce was a superb manipulator of material—perhaps the greatest. He was making words do the absolute maximum of work. . . . The kind of work I do is one in which I'm not master of my material. The more Joyce knew the more he could. He's tending toward omniscience and omnipotence as an artist. I'm working with impotence, ignorance. I don't think impotence has been exploited in the past. There seems to be a kind of esthetic axiom that expression is an achievement—must be an achievement. My little exploration is that whole zone of being that has always been set aside by artists as something unuseable—as something by definition incompatible with art.[9]

Both master and disciple strained the limits of art: Joyce trying to get everything in, to relate it all; Beckett trying to empty out and get

[9] Shenker, *New York Times,* p. 3.

rid of everything. Failing in reaching their opposed absolute ends, they were alike in finding absolute endlessness.

An author who seeks in each work to write the last word, who never knows where the next work is coming from, and who is convinced that he cannot follow himself should not be expected to father a school. Those who resemble him somewhat cease doing so when they cannot withstand the temptation of vitality, or meaning, or change. Only perhaps his compatriots by adoption—his great admirer Robbe-Grillet and his colleague in the New Novel, Nathalie Sarraute—show kinship to Beckett in their desire to omit all that is not certain and even to cast doubt on that which is included. But with these writers we appreciate reduction only intellectually, whereas in Beckett this is accompanied by something like emotional gratitude. Robbe-Grillet and Sarraute simplify their task and our experience by beginning with man dehumanized, while Beckett makes us feel man's struggle with his own dehumanization as if it were happening for the first time and at every moment. And simultaneously—only with Beckett—we feel the pressure of a bizarre, audacious humor. Inexplicably, even while all certainty about character is denied, Beckett's work preserves an ineluctable human content. Perhaps this is the indomitable Irish strain thrusting itself forth through the fierce French rigor. Or perhaps it is in an indisputably positive sense a case of the main drift of human experience expressing itself through Beckett miraculously without detail.

When the early draft of *Fin de Partie* is contrasted with the finished French version, and that in turn with Beckett's English translation, we see again the process of reduction which characterizes Beckett's career. In a letter to Alan Schneider written on January 11, 1956, Beckett first mentioned working on a new two-act play, and on April 12, wrote that he didn't like it: "It has turned out a three-legged giraffe, to mention only the architectonics, and leaves me in doubt whether to take a leg off or add one on." [10] By June he had trimmed the beast to the one-act *Fin de Partie* we have. Ruby Cohn has offered a useful account of the early two-act version now in the Ohio State University library.[11] She notes that its action is much more busy and various. Not only does Nell clearly die at the end of Act I, not only are there more props, more items of conversation, more colors (faces fade from red to white between acts), but also, through disguise,

[10] This and other letters to Schneider here quoted appeared in *The Village Voice*, March 19, 1958, pp. 8, 15.

[11] "The Beginning of *Endgame*," *Modern Drama* IX (December, 1966), 319–23.

Clov introduces two fresh characters. The first appears as a consequence of Clov's reading aloud from the Bible about Noah's flood and the large families descending from Shem. Moved to procreate also, Hamm orders a woman from Clov, who reenters with wig, breasts, skirt and a woman's voice, to obscenely comic effect. Later, after sighting the boy, Clov comes on stage in childish costume, complaining of hunger like the man in Hamm's chronicle, and learns to run Hamm's errands. In the revision the action shrinks so that the words, greatly reduced in number, may get our concentrated attention. Miss Cohn compares *Endgame* with *Godot* in its mode of reiteration: "The two acts of *Godot* resemble each other as do the days of our lives. In *Endgame* life is precipitated to a single day in which minute details resemble each other repetitively—phrase, gesture, and pause." [12] Biblical allusions are subtler, the theatrical metaphor more pronounced, and general verbal repetition is particularly heightened in the one-act version, enforcing our sense of the inadequacy of words, enforcing what Beckett called "the power of the text to claw." [13]

Beckett waited a year to translate *Fin de Partie* and then wrote on April 30, 1957, with misgivings to Schneider that it would "inevitably be a poor substitute for the original (the loss will be much greater than from the French to the English 'Godot')." "Loss" may well be as ambivalent a word in Beckett's vocabulary as "impossibility" is. For the most conspicuous loss in the translation is like that in the cutting of *Fin de Partie* to one act—a loss of variety and a further narrowing of the verbal range. Thus where the French version sometimes substitutes "achevé" and "cassé" for the opening word "fini," in English it is "finished" throughout. Similarly, the iterated "Zero" and "Once!" are more insisted upon in English, and, where the French still varied slightly, Beckett creates refrains in English with Clov's sardonic "Lucky for you," and Hamm's "Outside of here it's death." Having written to Schneider on June 21, 1956, that the play in French was "more inhuman than 'Godot,' " he now deepens this sense and harshens Nell's "comédie" into "farce," and Clov's offering of the gaff with *"Avale-la"* to *"Stick it up."* Although the English version pursues further the deliberate stage-consciousness—introducing the line, "Not an underplot" and rendering "Finie la rigolade" in an echo of Shakespeare's Prospero as "Our revels now are ended"—sheer word play is sacrificed in other instances. Because of all this, one imagines that as Beckett was perhaps first moved to tackle French to minimize the dis-

[12] *Ibid.*, p. 319.

[13] Letter to Schneider, June 21, 1956.

tracting quality of suggestiveness of the English tongue, he seeks out of sheer discipline to minimize it further in returning to English. This seems to me the best explanation of his cutting of the passage about the boy which Martin Esslin and Hugh Kenner discuss, since it is precisely the allusions to Jesus, Moses, and Buddha that are excised. If the French passage is a rough equivalent of Godot's hopeful sprouting tree, Beckett in English resists the seduction of such implicit interpretation. He follows *within* the play his general rule about criticism of his play, as he put it to Schneider on December 29, 1957:

> I feel the only line is to refuse to be involved in exegesis of any kind. And to insist on the extreme simplicity of dramatic situation and issue. If that's not enough for them, and it obviously isn't, it's enough for us, and we have no elucidations to offer of mysteries that are all of their making. My work is a matter of fundamental sounds (no joke intended) made as fully as possible, and I accept responsibility for nothing else. If people want to have headaches among the overtones, let them. And provide their own aspirin.

Some such caveat seems at the back of the minds of most of the critics here represented. Whether concerned, as Esslin and Goldman are, with the critical approach the play requires, or with its network of allusions as Cohn is, or with its peculiar genre as Kenner and Easthope are, or with its philosophical drive as Chambers is, all respond in some way to the play's quality of resistance. Since, despite their differences, all of these essays treat the play primarily as a dramatic text to be grappled with, I have flanked them with two very different sorts of account. The first, by Beckett's American director and friend, Schneider, is of the most concrete sort. The last, by the profoundly interdisciplinary thinker and social critic, Adorno, is of the most abstract and vast. It balances the more special approaches of the rest of the book with a very different sort of criticism, bringing to bear as it does contemporary Western history, art, and thought. Since Adorno adopts a dialectical method, while acknowledging the breakdown of all systems in which such a method has been rooted, his essay is necessarily difficult, a series of analytic forays and extended critical comparisons. By virtue precisely of its "fundamental sounds" *Endgame* becomes here a tool by which the losses of contemporary life may be assessed. According to Adorno, the play is poised equally between the outmoded requirements of a realism such as the socialist critic Georg Lukacs urges and the goals of Existentialism, whose "radical questions" are implicitly shown by Beckett to be loaded. Attacking thus the meaning of objectivity and subjectivity, Beckett exposes the bankrupt assumptions of rationality itself. This is the ultimate sense in which Beckett is, as Ionesco calls him, *"le véritable démystificateur."* [14] Thus Adorno's essay reveals that, despite the infinite regression from time and space, history and relevance, which I have discussed here, and because of the profound seriousness of that retreat, we are given a work which poses the fiercest challenge to everything by which we try to live.

[14] *L'Express,* June 1, 1961, p. 43.

Waiting for Beckett: A Personal Chronicle

by Alan Schneider

I take no sides. I am interested in the shape of ideas. There is a wonderful sentence in Augustine: "Do not despair; one of the thieves was saved. Do not presume; one of the thieves was damned." That sentence has a wonderful shape. It is the shape that matters.

SAMUEL BECKETT

In the three years that I have come to know him, the shape of Samuel Beckett as a human being has come to matter as much to me as do his plays. Perhaps even more. For Beckett is that most uncompromised of men, one who writes—and lives—as he must, and not as the world—and the world's critics—want him to. An artist, who works with no fears of "failure," which has fed him most of his writing life, or any expectation of "success," which has only lately greeted him. A friend, who has come unannounced to see me off at the Gare du Nord although I had not informed him which of the numerous trains to London I might be taking. The head of a physics or math professor set atop the torso and legs of a quarter-miler; a paradoxical combination of a Frenchman's fundamental "commitment" to life and an Irishman's basic good nature. Such is the shape of the man who has written some of the most terrifying and beautiful prose of the twentieth century.

* * *

[Schneider relates his discovery of *En Attendant Godot* in Paris, his meeting with Beckett, his attempt to produce *Godot* in Miami in January, 1956, and its failure and abandonment there. In Paris he met Beckett again.]

From "Waiting for Beckett: A Personal Chronicle" by Alan Schneider. From Chelsea Review, *no. 2 (September, 1958), 3, 9–17, 19–20.*

What he made me understand most of all was that he appreciated my concern with his work, that the actual results in Miami didn't matter, that failure in the popular sense was something he had breathed in all his life, and that the only thing which counted was one's own sense of achievement, one's own need to be honest with oneself. No other playwright whom I have ever known could have been so simply and so unselfconsciously unselfish. I would have done anything for Sam.

My opportunity was not long in coming. That new play he was working on was taking shape and had been scheduled for presentation in Paris in the spring of 1957. *Fin de Partie* it was called, again with only four characters (two of them popping out of ashcans) and a special world of its own. The New York press, intrigued by *Godot,* began to publish tidbits about the new play, saying that it was even more "weird," that it dealt with two men buried up to their necks in wet sand, etc. The title came to be translated as *The End of the Game* and even *The Game Is Up* instead of its proper *Endgame,* as in the last section of a game of chess. Eventually, as it turned out, the French production lost its theatre because of a timid management, and had its premiere (in French) only through the good offices of the Royal Court in London. Then another management took it over and it ran in Paris through the fall. The London critics, with the exception of Harold Hobson, were even more baffled and negative than they had been with *Godot*; even Tynan confessed his deep disappointment with the newer play's special anatomy of melancholy. While the French critics were, as usual, fervently and hopelessly divided.

Sam had sent me a copy of the French text which I tried, without success, to have someone translate for me. But I didn't have to read every line to know how I felt. One day, I sent him a cable asking for the rights to present the play off-Broadway, where I felt it would reach its proper audience. I had secured the agreement of Noel Behn, manager of the Cherry Lane, one of the best and most intimate of off-Broadway theatres, to present *Endgame* there as soon as its current occupant, Sean O'Casey's *Purple Dust,* had concluded its run; that would probably be around the first of the year. And the reason I wanted to option the play myself was in order to maintain what I felt was a necessary amount of artistic control over all the elements of production, a condition which I had not been able to obtain in my previous encounter with a Beckett play. Fate was knocking at my door for the second time—but this time I was furnishing some of the elbow-grease.

All spring and into the summer I corresponded with Sam and his New York publisher and agent, Barney Rosset of Grove Press, about the arrangements to be made. Although, as Sam said, he felt strange about negotiating for an English translation which did not yet exist. Eventually, after many weeks, it did exist, eventually it came, and eventually—and with a sense of real anticipation—I sat down one evening to read "the ashcan play," as it had generally become known by this time. In fact, it was only with the greatest of difficulty that we could get the press to understand that the two chief characters were *not* in ashcans.

Though I came to *Endgame* in exactly the opposite manner in which I had been introduced to *Godot,* via the text rather than in the theatre, the experience was equally impressive. Of course, I had come more prepared this time: two years of contact with Sam, a reading and re-reading of all his novels, and of everything I could find that had been written about his work. Whatever the reasons, I found myself literally bowled over by the scope and intensity of the new play's material. Not that I understood everything Sam was driving at; the text was much more taut and elliptical than *Godot*'s. But I was certainly carried away with the theatrical powers and possibilities of this alternately terrifying and uproarious, horrible and beautiful, tone-poem. The gentle aged couple in the ashcans was, of course, a marvelous invention and yet completely organic to the theme. But equally fascinating were the two central figures: the blind, majestic, and yet ever-so-human tyrant Hamm, and his shambling automaton attendant Clov. Frankly, I didn't spend much time worrying what all this "meant" or "was about"—whether it was the last four people left on earth after an atomic explosion; or the older generation being tossed on the ashheap by the younger; or, as someone suggested, Pozzo and Lucky in the third act of *Godot.* Just as *Godot* dealt with a promised arrival that never took place, so *Endgame* dealt with a promised and unfulfilled departure. More than anything else, it seemed to me to be, in a sense, a kind of tragic poem, man's last prayer to a God that might or might not exist. Far from depressing me, it lifted me out of myself, exhilarated me, provided a dramatic experience as strong as the one I had when I first discovered *Oedipus* or *Lear.* And what most delighted me was that in *Endgame* were more of Sam's special gifts for language and rhythm, for making the sublime ridiculous and the ridiculous sublime.

In fact, I wrote to Barney Rosset that the part of Hamm needed a combination Oedipus, Lear, and Hamlet—a neat trick of casting even at Broadway rates, much less off-Broadway. Nevertheless I was determined to try. And, more importantly, Sam was willing to have me try.

With our arrangements for New York production completed, Sam was anxious that I see the Paris version before it closed at the end of

October. No more anxious than I. For, once more, I had stored up a fund of questions which could best be answered in person. Luckily, the manager of the Cherry Lane agreed. A trans-Atlantic voyage is a sizeable item in an off-Broadway budget. But in this case a vital one. So in October I was off on my second pilgrimage to Beckett, this time overnight and by air directly to Paris.

As it happened, Sam and I missed each other at the Gare des Invalides on my arrival, but met at the hotel—this time a modest one in Montparnasse (as befitted off-Broadway). For a week, we met every day and for most of the day, taking long walks (one lovely sunny afternoon we polished off a pound of grapes while strolling through the Luxembourg Gardens), having lunch and dinner together, inhabiting various cafes at all hours. The French production of *Endgame,* after a run of almost 100 performances, was in its last week; I saw it four times, once while following the English translation with an usher's flashlight until the usher politely told me I was bothering the actors. I spoke with the French cast, especially director Roger Blin, who played Hamm so magnificently; and was able to check on all the technical details of the production. The Paris production had been basically as Sam wanted it, although like all practicing playwrights he was gradually discovering that all actors have personalities and get ideas which may seriously affect the intentions of the author. Again Sam tried to answer all my questions, no matter how stupid they seemed to him—or how often I asked them. "What were Clov's visions?" "Who was that mysterious Mother Pegg that kept cropping up?" "What did it mean for Hamm's and Clove's faces to be red, while Nagg's and Nell's were white?" (As Sam counter-asked, why was Werther's coat green? Because the author saw it that way.)

Each time I read the script or saw the play performed, I had a flock of new questions. Sam was always patient and ever tolerant; he wanted to help all he could. And he helped me more than I can ever say or even know. When I left for home, I knew *Endgame* a hundred times better than when I had arrived, knew what Hamm should look like and sound like, knew how best the ashcans should be placed, knew how carefully and how exactly I'd have to work on its rhythms and tones. As for its larger meanings, gradually the mosaic was falling into place, its design still shadowy but perceivable and inevitable.

The main question—contrary to the one I was generally asked: Which play did I like better, *Godot* or *Endgame*?—was: Who in New York could and would play Hamm? In Paris, Blin had given a bravura classic performance in the grand manner, such as only the French theatre could still offer. George Devine, whom I had seen and admired many times, was scheduled to play the role in London; he was excellent casting. What we needed was something of the calibre of Paul Muni—who was seriously ill—or Charles Laughton—who was abroad. I left Paris and Sam's last piece of advice: "Do it the way you like, Alan, do it ahny way you like!" feeling that somewhere there was bound to be a Hamm—if only we could find him.

Look for him we did! For over two months, the actors streamed in and out of the Cherry Lane offices, and the telephones rang all over New York. Our first choices for the parents were P. J. Kelly and Nydia Westman—and we were fortunate in interesting both. To this day, I can scarcely visualise anyone other than P. J. and Nydia in those ash-cans. For Clov, we had several strong choices, depending for our final selection on what kind of Hamm we were to find. Hamm himself remained unobtainable. Muni was indeed not to be had. Laughton wrote us a letter saying he was fascinated by the play but would rather have had Ilse Koch make him into a lampshade than play that part! Others were intrigued but not available, or available but not intrigued; still others interested but somehow not suited. We despaired, postponed, kept looking.

At last, after a brief trial with another actor, we came up with what turned out to be an extremely fortunate choice: a young and relatively unknown performer, Lester Rawlins, with whom I had worked in Washington some years back and who since coming to New York had had his considerable talents hidden behind a succession of Shakespearean beards. For Clov, we took Alvin Epstein, a specialist in mime and the "Lucky" of the New York *Godot.* (He was later succeeded by Gerald Hiken, not available at the time we were opening, who gave an equally fine performance.) Rawlins had a very low-pitched and flexible voice of great timbre, an imposing presence, and a countenance like granite; at times, he would remind me physically of Blin, yet he succeeded in making the role uniquely and powerfully his own. Epstein's stage movement was always arresting and carefully realised. And Nell and Nagg were adorable. The first hurdle had been well jumped, now we were on our way.

The day after New Year's 1958, we went into rehearsal. First rehearsals of a new play are always a kind of adventure into the unknown, a stepping out into uncharted space. This is especially true of a Beckett play, where so many of the standard conventions are broken or ignored—the beginning, the middle and end of an organised plot-line, clear-cut character progression, dramatic mobility and color—and yet so many new ones laid down—tones, rhythms, and cross-currents of relationship, which the author has built into the very fibre of his material. No other author I know of writes stage directions which are so essentially and specifically valid—as we discovered to our gain on each occasion when we ventured to disregard or to oppose them. His pauses are as much a part of the text as the words themselves. And I soon found myself not only getting more and more faithful to his printed demands but expecting an equal allegiance from the actors when they tended to go off on their own tangents—as actors are wont to do.

As well as designers. Our setting was being designed by a talented newcomer, David Hays, whose reputation was largely based on his designs for O'Neill's *Long Day's Journey into Night* and *The Iceman Cometh.* I made the mistake of showing him photographs of the Paris production, whereupon he tried to do everything exactly differently. After he had submitted several designs, all of which were rejected, we discovered that the stone-and-brick walls of the Cherry Lane stage were marvelously available and suited to represent Hamm and Clov's "shelter"—even to the extent of having a doorway at exactly the proper location for Clov's "kitchen." This discovery provided us with a most useful and authentic interior whose actual walls and floor produced sound of great effectiveness and which could be lit well and simply. How to manage the windows posed our only problem; eventually—and with Sam's wholehearted approval—we painted them, complete with window frames, boldly and theatrically on the wall at the back. (One part of the frame was made practical to allow for its opening near the end of the play.) No one minded in the slightest except those who looked for additional philosophical overtones from two painted windows on a bare brick wall.

Not that we shied away from all "significance" or meaning. But I have long ago discovered that the director's function is not so much to explain the author's meaning to his actors—whose problem of expressing that meaning to the audience is not necessarily helped by intellectually understanding it—but to see that, through whatever theatrical means, the actors are led to *do* those things which will *result* in the author's meaning being expressed. No actors can act out the *meaning* of *Endgame*—or any other play. They can and did act the roles of the various characters in the various situations and moments and relationships which Beckett had provided for them. They acted them with interest and variety, I hope, and with a sense of form but always as actual people in an actual situation. Beckett himself had always stressed that he was writing about what he termed a "local situation," i.e., Hamm and Clov (as well as Nagg and Nell) were individual personalities operating in a given set of circumstances. They were not to be considered as abstractions or symbols, or as representing anything other than themselves. After that, if the audience—or the critics—wanted to look for significance of some kind, let them do so, at their own initiative—and peril.

I found, for example, that it became convenient for me to suggest to the actors that the relation of Hamm and Clov could be likened to that of the mind and the body, the intellectual and the physical faculties, inseparable and yet always in conflict. But I never meant that I thought they *were* the mind and the body, or that that was what Sam intended. It was simply a theatrical means of leading the actors into certain areas of creativity and imagination. And definitely more helpful than figuring out whether the names of Hamm and Clov meant ham and cloves, or the Biblical Ham and the cloven foot, and a dozen other secret codes—all of which were obviously irrelevant.

Fortunately, the actors were most cooperative. Nydia Westman, for one, though occasionally or often baffled by what she had to do or say, strove valiantly and with all good will to carry out what I asked her to do. P. J. Kelly, who in his seventy-eight years had had many similar experiences, especially, as he confessed, with Irish playwrights, was equally agreeable. And they both coped good-naturedly with the numerous practical problems involved in making entrances and exits and spending an entire evening in two non-custom-made ashcans. While Rawlins and Epstein, one of whom never left his armchair and the other never allowed to rest from the burden of a constantly uncomfortable stance, did all in their power to carry out their respective jobs as I kept saying—and feeling—Sam would have wanted them to.

By the time we were well into rehearsals, the Cherry Lane management—joined by an optimistic trio known as Rooftop Productions—had no illusions about my initial responsibility being to the author. A number of times during this period, one or the other would get worried that I was making the play "too serious." They occasionally urged me to "gag it up" a bit here and there—which I refused to do, especially since I felt that the production abounded with legitimate laughter. Once or twice, I believe they became upset about one or the other of the performances—or about what I was doing with them. Had I not retained that much coveted artistic control by the very terms of my contract, I might have been forced to make fundamental changes with which I was completely in disagreement—or risked being fired. As it was, I resisted all attempts to change or distort what Sam had written, or go against any of the things he had confided in me during my Paris sojourn and in subsequent letters.

Personally, I felt rehearsals were going extremely well; the texture of Sam's writing was gradually emerging, rich in both its serious and comedic elements. Cast morale was high. Their dedication to the enterprise was really remarkable, especially in view of the nominal salaries they were getting and the general lack of glamour of off-Broadway. Interest on the part of the public was also considerable if not tremendous, though we were not getting as much publicity as we wanted. Throughout, I kept constantly in touch with Sam, letting him know all our ups and downs, and continuing to question him in detail—his answers always opening up new vistas and new possibilities.

* * *

[Schneider describes the enthusiasm of preview audiences, the relative coolness of the crowd on opening night (when the steam pipes banged during performance), the respectful review of Walter Kerr, the excellent notice of Brooks Atkinson, and the play's general success.]

Beckett's plays stay in the bones. They haunt me sleeping and waking, coming upon me when I am least aware. Sometimes a stray bit of conversation heard by accident on a bus or in a restaurant brings home one of Vladimir's and Estragon's "little canters." Sometimes I find myself actually reacting like Clov or like Hamm or, more often, like both simultaneously. Sam's characters seem to me always more alive and more truly lasting than those in the slice-of-life realistic dramas with which our stages today abound. (They will be equally alive when most of those others are as dead as the characters in *The Great Divide.**) His words strike to the very marrow—the sudden sharp anguish of a Pozzo or of a Hamm crying out for understanding in an uncertain universe; Clov's detailed description of the bleak harsh landscape of our existence on earth. While against and in spite of the harshness and the uncertainty, there is the constant assertion of man's will, and spirit, his sense of humor, as the only bulwarks against despair; the constant "glimmers of hope," even in the dark depths of that abyss in which we find ourselves.

[Anticipating his work with *Krapp's Last Tape,* Schneider closes.]

* [A play by William Vaughn Moody, written in 1906.]

Samuel Beckett: The Search for the Self

by Martin Esslin

If *Waiting for Godot* shows its two heroes whiling away the time in a succession of desultory, and never-ending, games, Beckett's second play deals with an "endgame," the final game in the hour of death.

Waiting for Godot takes place on a terrifyingly empty open road, *Endgame* in a claustrophobic interior. *Waiting for Godot* consists of two symmetrical movements that balance each other; *Endgame* has only one act that shows the running down of a mechanism until it comes to a stop. Yet *Endgame,* like *Waiting for Godot,* groups its characters in symmetrical pairs.

In a bare room with two small windows, a blind old man, Hamm, sits in a wheelchair. Hamm is paralyzed, and can no longer stand. His servant, Clov, is unable to sit down. In two ash cans that stand by the wall are Hamm's legless parents, Nagg and Nell. The world outside is dead. Some great catastrophe, of which the four characters in the play are, or believe themselves to be, the sole survivors, has killed all living beings.

Hamm and Clov (ham actor and clown?) in some ways resemble Pozzo and Lucky. Hamm is the master, Clov the servant. Hamm is selfish, sensuous, domineering. Clov hates Hamm and wants to leave him, but he must obey his orders "Do this, do that, and I do it. I never refuse. Why?" [1] Will Clov have the force to leave Hamm? That is the source of the dramatic tension of the play. If he leaves, Hamm must die, as Clov is the only one left who can feed him. But Clov also must die, as there is no else left in the world, and Hamm's store is the last remaining source of food. If Clov can muster the will power to

---

From "Samuel Beckett: The Search for the Self." From The Theatre of the Absurd *by Martin Esslin (Garden City, New York: Doubleday & Company, Inc., 1961; London, Eyre & Spottiswoode [Publishers] Ltd., 1962), pp. 27–39.*

[1] Beckett, *Endgame* (New York: Grove Press, 1958), p. 43.

leave, he will not only kill Hamm but commit suicide. He will thus succeed where Estragon and Vladimir have failed so often.

Hamm fancies himself as a writer—or, rather, as the spinner of a tale of which he composes a brief passage every day. It is a story about a catastrophe that caused the death of large numbers of people. On this particular day, the tale has reached an episode in which the father of a starving child asks Hamm for bread for his child. Finally the father begs Hamm to take in his child, should it still be alive when he gets back to his home. It appears that Clov might well be that very child. He was brought to Hamm when he was too small to remember. Hamm was a father to him, or, as he himself puts it, "But for me . . . no father. But for Hamm . . . no home." [2] The situation in *Endgame* is the reverse of that in Joyce's *Ulysses,* where a father finds a substitute for a lost son. Here a foster son is trying to leave his foster father.

Clov has been trying to leave Hamm ever since he was born, or as he says, "Ever since I was whelped." [3] Hamm is burdened with a great load of guilt. He might have saved large numbers of people who begged him for help. "The place was crawling with them!" [4] One of the neighbors, old Mother Pegg, who was "bonny once, like a flower of the field" and perhaps Hamm's lover, was killed through his cruelty: "When old Mother Pegg asked you for oil for her lamp and you told her to get out to hell . . . you know what she died of, Mother Pegg? Of darkness." [5] Now the supplies in Hamm's own household are running out: the sweets, the flour for the parents' pap, even Hamm's painkiller. The world is running down. "Something is taking its course." [6]

Hamm is childish; he plays with a three-legged toy dog, and he is full of self-pity. Clov serves him as his eyes. At regular intervals he is asked to survey the outside world from the two tiny windows high up in the wall. The right-hand window looks out on land, the left-hand onto the sea. But even the tides have stopped.

Hamm is untidy. Clov is a fanatic of order.

Hamm's parents, in their dustbins, are grotesquely sentimental imbeciles. They lost their legs in an accident while cycling through the Ardennes on their tandem, on the road to Sedan. They remember the day they went rowing on Lake Como—the day after they became en-

[2] Ibid., p. 38.
[3] Ibid., p. 14.
[4] Ibid., p. 68.
[5] Ibid., p. 75.
[6] Ibid., p. 13.

gaged—one April afternoon (cf. the love scene in a boat on a lake in *Krapp's Last Tape*), and Nagg, in the tones of an Edwardian raconteur, retells the funny story that made his bride laugh then and that he has since repeated *ad nauseam*.

Hamm hates his parents. Nell secretly urges Clov to desert Hamm. Nagg, having been awakened to listen to Hamm's tale, scolds him: "Whom did you call when you were a tiny boy, and were frightened in the dark? Your mother? No. Me." But he immediately reveals how selfishly he ignored these calls.

> We let you cry. Then we moved out of earshot, so that we might sleep in peace. . . . I hope the day will come when you'll really need to have me listen to you. . . . Yes, I hope I'll live till then, to hear you calling me like when you were a tiny little boy, and were frightened, in the dark, and I was your only hope.[7]

As the end approaches, Hamm imagines what will happen when Clov leaves him. He confirms Nagg's forecast: "There I'll be in the old shelter, alone against the silence and . . . the stillness. . . . I'll have called my father and I'll have called my . . . my son," [8] which indicates that he does indeed regard Clov as his son.

For a last time, Clov looks out of the windows with his telescope. He sees something unusual. "A small . . . boy!" But it is not entirely clear whether he has really seen this strange sign of continuing life, "a potential procreator." [9] In some way, this is the turning point. Hamm says, "It's the end, Clov, we've come to the end. I don't need you any more." [10] Perhaps he does not believe that Clov will really be able to leave him. But Clov has finally decided that he will go: "I open the door of the cell and go. I am so bowed I only see my feet, if I open my eyes, and between my legs a little trail of black dust. I say to myself that the earth is extinguished, though I never saw it lit. . . . It's easy going. . . . When I fall I'll weep for happiness." [11] And as blind Hamm indulges in a last monologue of reminiscene and self-pity, Clov appears, dressed for departure in a Panama hat, tweed coat, raincoat over his arm, and listens to Hamm's speech, motionless. When the curtain falls, he is still there. It remains open whether he will really leave.

The final tableau of *Endgame* bears a curious resemblance to the ending of a little-known but highly significant play by the brilliant Russian dramatist and man of the theatre Nikolai Evreinov, which

[7] Ibid., p. 56.
[8] Ibid., p. 69.
[9] Ibid., p. 78.
[10] Ibid., p. 79.
[11] Ibid., p. 81.

appeared in an English translation as early as 1915—*The Theatre of the Soul.*[12] This one-act play is a monodrama that takes place *inside a human being* and shows the constituent parts of his ego, his emotional self and his rational self in conflict with each other. The man, Ivanov, is sitting in a café, debating with himself whether to run away with a night-club singer or go back to his wife. His emotional self urges him to leave, his rational self tries to persuade him of the advantages, moral and material, of staying with his wife. As they come to blows, a bullet pierces the heart that has been beating in the background. Ivanov has shot himself. The rational and emotional selves fall down dead. A third figure, who has been sleeping in the background, gets up. He is dressed in traveling clothes and carries a suitcase. It is the immortal part of Ivanov that now has to move on.

While it is unlikely that Beckett knew this old and long-forgotten Russian play, the parallels are very striking. Evreinov's monodrama is a purely rational construction designed to present to a cabaret audience what was then the newest psychological trend. Beckett's play springs from genuine depths. Yet the suggestion that *Endgame* may also be a monodrama has much to be said for it. The enclosed space with the two tiny windows through which Clov observes the outside world; the dustbins that hold the suppressed and despised parents, and whose lids Clov is ordered to press down when they become obnoxious; Hamm, blind and emotional; Clov, performing the function of the senses for him—all these might well represent different aspects of a single personality, repressed memories in the subconscious mind, the emotional and the intellectual selves. Is Clov then the intellect, bound to serve the emotions, instincts, and appetites, and trying to free himself from such disorderly and tyrannical masters, yet doomed to die when its connection with the animal side of the personality is severed? Is the death of the outside world the gradual receding of the links to reality that takes place in the process of aging and dying? Is *Endgame* a monodrama depicting the dissolution of a personality in the hour of death?

It would be wrong to assume that these questions can be definitely answered. *Endgame* certainly was not planned as a sustained allegory of this type. But there are indications that there is an element of monodrama in the play. Hamm describes a memory that is strangely reminiscent of the situation in *Endgame*:

> I once knew a madman who thought the end of the world had come. He was a painter—an engraver. . . . I used to go and see him in the

[12] Nikolai Evreinov, *The Theatre of the Soul,* Monodrama, trans. M. Potapenko and C. St. John (London, 1915).

> asylum. I'd take him by the hand and drag him to the window. Look! There! All that rising corn! And there! Look! The sails of the herring fleet! All that loveliness! . . . He'd snatch away his hand and go back into his corner. Appalled. All he had seen was ashes. . . . He alone had been spared. Forgotten . . . It appears the case is . . . was not so . . . so unusual.[13]

Hamm's own world resembles the delusions of the mad painter. Moreover, what is the significance of the picture mentioned in the stage directions? "Hanging near door, its face to wall, a picture." [14] Is that picture a memory? Is the story a lucid moment in the consciousness of that very painter whose dying hours we witness from behind the scenes of his mind?

Beckett's plays can be interpreted on many levels. *Endgame* may well be a monodrama on one level and a morality play about the death of a rich man on another. But the peculiar psychological reality of Beckett's characters has often been noticed. Pozzo and Lucky have been interpreted as body and mind; Vladimir and Estragon have been seen as so complementary that they might be the two halves of a single personality, the conscious and the subconscious mind. Each of these three pairs—Pozzo-Lucky; Vladimir-Estragon; Hamm-Clov—is linked by a relationship of mutual interdependence, wanting to leave each other, at war with each other, and yet dependent on each other. "*Nec tecum, nec sine te.*" This is a frequent situation among people—married couples, for example—but it is also an image of the interrelatedness of the elements within a single personality, particularly if the personality is in conflict with itself.

In Beckett's first play, *Eleutheria,* the basic situation was, superficially, analogous to the relationship between Clov and Hamm. The young hero of that play wanted to leave his family; in the end he succeeded in getting away. In *Endgame,* however, that situation has been deepened into truly universal significance; it has been concentrated and immeasurably enriched precisely by having been freed from all elements of a naturalistic social setting and external plot. The process of contraction, which Beckett described as the essence of the artistic tendency in his essay on Proust, has here been carried out triumphantly. Instead of merely exploring a surface, a play like *Endgame* has become a shaft driven deep down into the core of being; that is why it exists on a multitude of levels, revealing new ones as it is more closely studied. What at first might have appeared as obscurity or lack of definition is later recognized as the very hallmark of

[13] *Endgame,* p. 44.
[14] Ibid., p. 1.

the density of texture, the tremendous concentration of a work that springs from a truly creative imagination, as distinct from a merely imitative one.

The force of these considerations is brought out with particular clarity when we are confronted by an attempt to interpret a play like *Endgame* as a mere exercise in conscious or subconscious autobiography. In an extremely ingenious essay[15] Lionel Abel has worked out the thesis that in the characters of Hamm and Pozzo, Beckett may have portrayed his literary master, James Joyce, while Lucky and Clov stand for Beckett himself. *Endgame* then becomes an allegory of the relationship between the domineering, nearly blind Joyce and his adoring disciple, who felt himself crushed by his master's overpowering literary influence. Superficially the parallels are striking: Hamm is presented as being at work on an interminable story, Lucky is being made to perform a set piece of thinking, which, Mr. Abel argues, is in fact a parody of Joyce's style. Yet on closer reflection this theory surely becomes untenable; not because there may not be a certain amount of truth in it (every writer is bound to use elements of his own experience of life in his work) but because, far from illuminating the full content of a play like *Endgame,* such an interpretation reduces it to a trivial level. If *Endgame* really were nothing but a thinly disguised account of the literary, or even the human, relationship between two particular individuals, it could not possibly produce the impact it has had on audiences utterly ignorant of these particular, very private circumstances. Yet *Endgame* undoubtedly has a very deep and direct impact, which can spring only from its touching a chord in the minds of a very large number of human beings. The problems of the relationship between a literary master and his pupil would be very unlikely to elicit such a response; very few people in the audience would feel directly involved. Admittedly, a play that presented the conflict between Joyce and Beckett openly, or thinly disguised, might arouse the curiosity of audiences who are always eager for autobiographical revelations. But this is just what *Endgame* does *not* do. If it nevertheless arouses profound emotion in its audience, this can be due only to the fact that it is felt to deal with a conflict of a far more universal nature. Once that is seen, it becomes clear that while it is fascinating to argue about the aptness of such autobiographical elements, such a discussion leaves the central problem of understanding the play and exploring its many-layered meanings still to be tackled.

As a matter of fact, the parallels are by no means so close: Lucky's

[15] Lionel Abel, "Joyce the Father, Beckett the Son," *The New Leader,* New York, December 14, 1959.

speech in *Waiting for Godot,* for example, is anything but a parody of Joyce's style. It is, if anything, a parody of philosophical jargon and scientific double-talk—the very opposite of what either Joyce or Beckett ever wanted to achieve in their writing. Pozzo, on the other hand, who would stand for Joyce, is utterly inartistic in his first persona, and becomes reflective in a melancholy vein only after he has gone blind. And if Pozzo is Joyce, what would be the significance of Lucky's dumbness, which comes at the same time as Pozzo's blindness? The novel that Hamm composes in *Endgame* is characterized by its attempt at scientific exactitude, and there is a clear suggestion that it is not a work of art at all, but a thinly disguised vehicle for the expression of Hamm's sense of guilt about his behavior at the time of the great mysterious calamity, when he refused to save his neighbors. Clov, on the other hand, is shown as totally uninterested in Hamm's "Work in Progress," so that Hamm has to bribe his senile father to listen to it—surely a situation as unlike that of Joyce and Beckett as can be imagined.

The experience expressed in Beckett's plays is of a far more profound and fundamental nature than mere autobiography. They reveal his experience of temporality and evanescence; his sense of the tragic difficulty of becoming aware of one's own self in the merciless process of renovation and destruction that occurs with change in time; of the difficulty of communication between human beings; of the unending quest for reality in a world in which everything is uncertain and the borderline between dream and reality is ever shifting; of the tragic nature of all love relationships and the self-deception of friendship (of which Beckett speaks in the essay on Proust), and so on. In *Endgame* we are also certainly confronted with a very powerful expression of the sense of deadness, of leaden heaviness and hopelessness, that is experienced in states of deep depression: the world outside goes dead for the victim of such states, but inside his mind there is ceaseless argument between parts of his personality that have become autonomous entities.

This is not to say that Beckett gives a clinical description of psychopathological states. His creative intuition explores the elements of experience and shows to what extent all human beings carry the seeds of such depression and disintegration within the deeper layers of their personality. If the prisoners of San Quentin responded to *Waiting for Godot,* it was because they were confronted with *their own experience* of time, waiting, hope, and despair; because they recognized the truth about *their own human relationships* in the sadomasochistic interdependence of Pozzo and Lucky and in the bickering hate-love between Vladimir and Estragon. This is also the key to the wide success of

Beckett's plays: to be confronted with concrete projections of the deepest fears and anxieties, which have been only vaguely experienced at a half-conscious level, constitutes a process of catharsis and liberation analogous to the therapeutic effect in psychoanalysis of confronting the subconscious contents of the mind. This is the moment of release from deadening habit, through facing up to the suffering of the reality of being, that Vladimir almost attains in *Waiting for Godot*. This also, probably, is the release that could occur if Clov had the courage to break his bondage to Hamm and venture out into the world, which may not, after all, be so dead as it appeared from within the claustrophobic confines of Hamm's realm. This, in fact, seems to be hinted at by the strange episode of the little boy whom Clov observes in the last stages of *Endgame*. Is this boy a symbol of life outside the closed circuit of withdrawal from reality?

It is significant that in the original, French version, this episode is dealt with in greater detail than in the later, English one. Again Beckett seems to have felt that he had been too explicit. And from an artistic point of view he is surely right; in his type of theatre the half-light of suggestion is more powerful than the overtly symbolical. But the comparison between the two versions is illuminating nevertheless. In the English version, Clov, after expressing surprise at what he has discovered, merely says:

> *Clov (dismayed)*. Looks like a small boy!
>
> *Hamm (sarcastic)*. A small . . . boy!
>
> *Clov*. I'll go and see. (*He gets down, drops the telescope, goes towards the door, turns.*) I'll take the gaff. (*He looks for the gaff, sees it, picks it up, hastens towards the door.*)
>
> *Hamm*. No!
>
> (*Clov halts.*)
>
> *Clov*. No? A potential procreator?
>
> *Hamm*. If he exists he'll die there or he'll come here. And if he doesn't . . . (*Pause.*)[16]

In the original, French version, Hamm shows far greater interest in the boy, and his attitude changes from open hostility to resignation.

> *Clov*. There is someone there! Someone!
>
> *Hamm*. Well, go and exterminate him! (*Clov gets down from the stool.*) Somebody! (*With trembling voice*) Do your duty! (*Clov rushes to the door.*) No, don't bother. (*Clov stops.*) What distance?
>
> (*Clov climbs back on the stool, looks through the telescope.*)
>
> *Clov*. Seventy . . . four meters.

[16] *Endgame*, p. 78.

Hamm. Approaching? Receding?

Clov (*continues to look*). Stationary.

Hamm. Sex?

Clov. What does it matter? (*He opens the window, leans out. Pause. He straightens, lowers the telescope, turns to Hamm, frightened.*) Looks like a little boy.

Hamm. Occupied with?

Clov. What?

Hamm (*violently*). What is he doing?

Clov (*also*). I don't know what he's doing. What little boys used to do. (*He looks through the telescope. Pause. Puts it down, turns to Hamm.*) He seems to be sitting on the ground, with his back against something.

Hamm. The lifted stone. (*Pause.*) Your eyesight is getting better. (*Pause.*) No doubt he is looking at the house with the eyes of Moses dying.

Clov. No.

Hamm. What is he looking at?

Clov (*violently*). I don't know what he is looking at. (*He raises the telescope. Pause. Lowers the telescope, turns to Hamm.*) His navel. Or thereabouts. (*Pause.*) Why this cross-examination?

Hamm. Perhaps he is dead.[17]

After this, the French text and the English version again coincide: Clov wants to tackle the newcomer with his gaff, Hamm stops him, and, after a brief moment of doubt as to whether Clov has told him the truth, realizes that the turning point has come:

> It's the end, Clov, we've come to the end. I don't need you any more.[18]

The longer, more elaborate version of this episode clearly reveals the religious or quasi-religious symbolism of the little boy; the references to Moses and the lifted stone seem to hint that the first human being, the first sign of life discovered in the outside world since the great calamity when the earth went dead, is not, like Moses, dying within sight of the promised land, but, like Christ the moment after the resurrection, has been newly born into a new life, leaning, a babe, against the lifted stone. Moreover, like the Buddha, the little boy contemplates his navel. And his appearance convinces Hamm that the moment of parting, the final stage of the endgame, has come.

It may well be that the sighting of this little boy—undoubtedly a climactic event in the play—stands for redemption from the illusion and evanescence of time through the recognition, and acceptance, of a higher reality: the little boy contemplates his own navel; that is, he

[17] Beckett, *Fin de Partie* (Paris: Les Editions de Minuit, 1957), pp. 103–5.
[18] *Endgame,* p. 79.

fixes his attention on the great emptiness of nirvana, nothingness, of which Democritus the Abderite has said, in one of Beckett's favorite quotations, "Nothing is more real than nothing." [19]

There is a moment of illumination, shortly before he himself dies, in which Murphy, having played a *game of chess,* experiences a strange sensation:

> . . . and Murphy began to see nothing, that colorlessness which is such a rare post-natal treat, being the absence . . . not of *percipere* but of *percipi.* His other senses also found themselves at peace, an unexpected pleasure. Not the numb peace of their own suspension, but the positive peace that comes when the somethings give way, or perhaps simply add up, to the Nothing, than which in the guffaw of the Abderite naught is more real. Time did not cease, that would be asking too much, but the wheels of rounds and pauses did, as Murphy with his head among the armies [i.e., of the chessmen] continued to suck in, through all the posterns of his withered soul, the accidentless One-and-Only conveniently called Nothing.[20]

Does Hamm, who has shut himself off from the world and killed the rest of mankind by holding on to his material possessions—Hamm, blind, sensual, egocentric—then die when Clov, the rational part of the self, perceives the true reality of the illusoriness of the material world, the redemption and resurrection, the liberation from the wheels of time that lies in union with the "accidentless One-and-Only, conveniently called Nothing"? Or is the discovery of the little boy merely a symbol of the coming of death—union with nothingness in a different, more concrete sense? Or does the reappearance of life in the outside world indicate that the period of loss of contact with the world has come to an end, that the crisis has passed and that a disintegrating personality is about to find the way back to integration, "the solemn change towards merciless reality in Hamm and ruthless acceptance of freedom in Clov," as the Jungian analyst Dr. Metman puts it? [21]

There is no need to try to pursue these alternatives any further; to decide in favor of one would only impair the stimulating coexistence of these and other possible implications. There is, however, an illuminating commentary on Beckett's views about the interrelation between material wants and a feeling of restlessness and futility in the short mime-play *Act Without Words,* which was performed with *Endgame* during its first run. The scene is a desert onto which a man is "flung

[19] Beckett, *Malone Dies,* in *Molloy. Malone Dies. The Unnameable* (London: John Calder, 1959), p. 193.

[20] *Murphy,* p. 246.

[21] Eva Metman, "Reflections on Samuel Beckett's Plays," *Journal of Analytical Psychology,* London, January, 1960, p. 58.

backwards." Mysterious whistles draw his attention in various directions. A number of more or less desirable objects, notably a carafe of water, are dangled before him. He tries to get the water. It hangs too high. A number of cubes, obviously designed to make it easier for him to reach the water, descend from the flies. But however ingeniously he piles them on top of one another, the water always slides just outside his reach. In the end he sinks into complete immobility. The whistle sounds—but he no longer heeds it. The water is dangled in front of his face—but he does not move. Even the palm tree in the shade of which he has been sitting is whisked off into the flies. He remains immobile, looking at his hands.[22]

Here again we find man flung onto the stage of life, at first obeying the call of a number of impulses, having his attention drawn to the pursuit of illusory objectives by whistles from the wings, but finding peace only when he has learned his lesson and refuses any of the material satisfactions dangled before him. The pursuit of objectives that forever recede as they are attained—inevitably so through the action of time, which changes us in the process of reaching what we crave—can find release only in the recognition of that nothingness which is the only reality. The whistle that sounds from the wings resembles the whistle with which Hamm summons Clov to minister to his material needs. And the final, immobile position of the man in *Act Without Words* recalls the posture of the little boy in the original version of *Endgame*.

The activity of Pozzo and Lucky, the driver and the driven, always on the way from place to place; the waiting of Estragon and Vladimir, whose attention is always focused on the promise of a coming; the defensive position of Hamm, who has built himself a shelter from the world to hold on to his possessions, are all aspects of the same futile preoccupation with objectives and illusory goals. All movement is disorder. As Clov says, "I love order. It's my dream. A world where all would be silent and still and each thing in its last place, under the last dust." [23]

[22] Beckett, *Act Without Words I*, in *Krapp's Last Tape and Other Dramatic Pieces* (New York: Grove Press, 1960).

[23] *Endgame*, p. 57.

Endgame and its Scorekeepers

by *Richard M. Goldman*

Samuel Beckett, in discussing the paintings of Bram van Velde,[1] has suggested that failure may be the proper province of the artist. Beckett's own work, resistant both to exegesis and to attempts to place it in a literary tradition, suggests that failure may also be the proper province of the critic. Since Beckett has aroused the interest of some of the most gifted contemporary critics, the result has been essays that are beautiful failures—and often beautifully aware of so being. Hugh Kenner is particularly sensitive to the fact that Beckett's work is always more than what can be made of it.[2] For we need to determine what kind of art Beckett is practising rather than translating his works into a set of meanings or placing them along the continuum of literary history.

Endgame provides the exegete with both field-day and dead-end. He may trace the chess metaphor, note the allusions to Shakespeare and Baudelaire, remark on the Christian reference; but, after he has done so, he finds himself with a variety of keys, new, old, some beautifully shaped, but with no locks to try them on. The mystery will not even define itself—let alone admit of solution. A number of critics have noted, for instance, that after Clov spots the young boy through his telescope, Hamm says to Clov: "I don't need you any more." Hamm regards the boy, these critics reason, as a possible replacement for Clov. The interpretation is not really suggestive, however. Hamm demonstrates no interest in the boy. He may not

---

[1] Samuel Beckett, in three dialogues with Georges Duthuit, appended to his *Proust* (London, 1965), p. 125.

[2] I am thinking particularly of this remarkable passage about *Godot*: "Throughout . . . we clutch at straws of meaning, persuaded at bottom only of one thing, that all four men exist, embodied, gravid, speaking; moving before us, their shadows cast on the wall, their voices echoing in the auditorium, their feet heavy on the boards." *Samuel Beckett* (New York, 1961), pp. 137–38.

need Clov because there is ever less food and medication for Clov to dole out. The "We've come to the end" which Hamm says immediately before "I don't need you any more" might betoken not only the end of their relationship but the end of their being—the end of the endgame, death. Moreover, Hamm is so anti-life throughout that the idea of a young boy with his life ahead of him might strike him as repugnant. The critics who attempt to link Clov's discovery through the telescope with Hamm's pronouncement are obeying the instinct of a mind trained to make meaningful connection, sure that such connection must be what the artist is after. But is he? The numerous indicated pauses in the play are utterly unlike the fraught silences in Harold Pinter's *The Homecoming*. There, the gaps are full of tension, electricity, strategy, and are hence connective. But those in *Endgame* are disjunctive—they mark a failure of reason, of energy, of attention. When speech resumes, the subject is changed. We are not meant to put two and two together.

Nor are we meant to knot Beckett with another writer; the knot slips. Beckett is often linked with Eugène Ionesco,[3] and *Endgame* with *The Chairs*.[4] But the plays are different in all respects save the textural. *The Chairs* moves toward the signal event, the appearance of the orator; while *Endgame* is devoid of event—the putative departure of Clov is a non-event, and despite a few critical attempts to suggest that its possibility is the source of the play's "suspense," its impossibility is stressed repeatedly ("There's no one else,"—"there's nowhere else"), and suspense is a dramatic virtue which one imagines Beckett would be unlikely to hang on. Indeed Beckett and Ionesco share little except their having come into prominence as *avant-gardistes* at about the same time. Ionesco's informing mode is metamorphosis (man into beast, inanimate into animate), while Beckett's is decay. Ionesco portrays the corruption of energy in *Rhinoceros* or the transference of energy in *The Lesson* while Beckett witnesses the inevitable loss of energy. Ionesco is unconventional in that he mocks convention or invents his own; Beckett jettisons convention, and, so much the lighter, his fragile barks move toward *rien,* zero, nothingness.

Nor do Beckett's plays make pleasant bedfellows with the works of earlier surrealists or dadaists or more recent serious playwrights or *avant-gardistes*. He is not *épatant* like Alfred Jarry or Roger Vitrac. His "black humor," unlike Jean Anouilh's, does not demonstrate the triumph of the insensitive over the sensitive or the corrupt over the

[3] The most sustained and successful attempt to forge this link can be found in Leonard Cabell Pronko's *Avant-Garde* (Berkeley, 1963), pp. 112–30.

[4] See Rosette Lamont's "The Metaphysical Farce: Beckett and Ionesco," *The French Review,* XXXII (February, 1957), 319–28.

pure. He does not forge myths to study the intersections of love and power like Jean Genet. He does not achieve counterpoint by subjecting an operetta-like plot to serious intellectual scrutiny in the manner of Georges Schehadé. There is none of the Spanish gothicism of Fernando Arrabal, the "theatre of cruelty" techniques of Arthur Adamov, the study of the authoritarian or police-state mentality of both Adamov and Michel de Ghelderode.

Beckett's work is no more comfortable in a diptych with T. S. Eliot's. Rosette Lamont's brilliant suggestion that Hamm is a Fisher-King, Clov a Parsifal, the Grail a jar of dry cookies, creates waves of new possibility.[5] Eliot is, after all, the poet of diminution, and might not Beckett further diminish his images? Soon, however, the waves break. One recalls that *The Waste Land* is minatory and didactic, modes remote from Beckett's, that the shards which Eliot holds up to the light were once part of a whole—a golden bowl now broken in a sacred grove now a desert—while the shards that fill Beckett's plays seem to have been *created* as such. All references to the past in his plays never convince us that the characters or their world were ever different. Hamm may have once been mobile; Nagg and Nell may have once been in love on Lake Como; Winnie in *Happy Days* may not always have been buried in sand—but can one *imagine* them in any save their present estate? The word "once" denoting a *temps perdu* echoes through *Endgame.* "You loved me once," Hamm insists to Clov. The sand in the ashcan was "once" sawdust, Nagg reminds Nell. Mother Pegg was "bonny once," Hamm muses, but Clov impatiently interrupts: "We too were bonny—once. It's a rare thing not to have been bonny—once." The very repetition of the word seems to mock as sentimental the notion that life was once richer. Clov intones at the end: "I say to myself that the earth is extinguished though I never saw it lit." Nor is there a sense of a future that one finds in Eliot. While Eliot looks away from a human spring to a Second Coming, Beckett looks away from a human winter toward the loss of all motion and being.

Nor is Beckett a dramatizer of the philosopher's position although his art has been termed "existential." The plays of modern French philosophers like Sartre and Camus, while they move away from moral and psychological systems that exist outside of and prior to the individual confrontation, cleave nevertheless to a pattern of action and consequence. Beckett, however, has abolished the individual confrontation and the action-consequence pattern. The existentialist notion of "autonomy" is foreign to Beckett's world in which there is either

[5] Lamont, p. 326.

slavery to another man or slavery to *being* man. Moreover, while the debate about existentialism centers around the claims to priority of essence and existence, there are no priorities in Beckett's plays—he writes about the essence of existence—life departicularized, its processes (maturation, willed change) cut off; its contexts (moral, psychological) abrogated; its battles (authority versus freedom, good versus evil) not joined by either side. There is a sense neither of nationality (is Vladimir in *Godot* Russian? Estragon, Spanish?) nor, although some commentators find the *angst* of a post-atomic age in his work, of era. The characters do not work for a living (removing them from the middle class) or procreate (removing them from all classes). The world has been reduced.

Endgame carries this reduction a step further than *Waiting for Godot.* It dispenses with the appointment that gives an illusory *telos* to the earlier play. It narrows the types of human relationship. The two pairs of men in *Godot* represent two basic kinds of relationship: Gogo and Didi a friendship; Pozzo and Lucky, a power relationship. In *Endgame* the relationship between Hamm and Clov is seemingly both but actually neither. Hamm and Clov have all the preconditions of friendship. Their names suggest substance and its perfect seasoning; their faces are red, unlike the white faces of Nagg and Nell; they share the fate of a growing disability. But they are not friends.[6] They play the "endgame" against each other, and while Gogo and Didi have moments of tenderness, Hamm and Clov share only the grudging respect paid to a clever opponent. Nor are they master and slave. Clov is not tethered as was Lucky; he is free to go—were there a place to go. Friendship and power have ceased to mean anything to these creatures. The only relationship possible for them is symbiosis, expressed here not as what each animal can do that the other cannot, but what each cannot do—Hamm cannot stand; Clov cannot sit. As partners of a symbiosis, their relationship seems biological and prehuman. As red chess men, their relationship seems extra-human. As figures in the tableau that opens and closes the play, they seem parahuman. Yet, mysteriously, their relationship, in its very shifting of definition and its ultimate failure of definition, seems quite human indeed.

If neither man is defined by his complex and unnamable relation to the other, neither can be fixed and formulated in a moral phrase. The most frequent critical allegation against Hamm is that he is cruel. This

[6] Readers interested in the motif of friendship in Beckett's work should consult his remarks about Proust's attitude toward friendship which seems congruent with his own: "Proust situates friendship somewhere between fatigue and ennui." *Proust,* pp. 64–65

cruelty is apparent and yet unreal. He does threaten to give Clov no more to eat, but Clov triumphs over the threat with crooked yet potent logic. If he is denied all food, Clov argues, he will die—a release, hence no cruelty. Hamm counters that he will allow Clov just enough food to live and be miserable. Then Clov reasons, he will not die—a reprieve, hence no cruelty. Hamm cannot triumph any more than a villain in a pantomime can—and stage villainy (rhetoric, not action) is his style. "Accursed progenitor," he calls his father, but the phrase is so operatic that the exegete begins to thumb through his *bel canto libretti,* wondering if some *tenore* might not have called some *basso "genitore maledetto";* the phrase is too extravagant to be cruel. Nor can one accuse Hamm of placing his parents in ashcans. We do not know how they got there; they are simply there. Even Clov's sudden accusation that Hamm was responsible for the death of Mother Pegg carries no weight. Mother Pegg had asked Hamm for oil for her lamp and had been denied. Clov plays it up: "You know what she died of, Mother Pegg? Of darkness." There is a moment of tension, but it cannot sustain itself. There is a pause, long enough for us to wonder: "Who was Mother Pegg? Can one *die* of darkness—in its physical or even metaphoric sense?" The dialogue resumes: does Clov have his telescope, Hamm queries. The charge is clearly not going to be pressed. Like Hamm's own epithet, it is too extravagant to stick. The evidence is overwhelming, but the verdict is "innocent."

Indeed, one can argue (wrongly) that Clov is the more cruel. He denies Hamm the forgiveness he frequently seeks; he denies him the small comforts of being either pathetic (when Hamm cries "Nature has forgotten us," Clov counters with, "There is no more nature," and when Hamm insists that nature is present in the fact that they are decaying, Clov points out, "Then she hasn't forgotten us") or courageous (when Hamm's momentarily stiff upper lip proclaims, "We do what we can," Clov responds, "We shouldn't"). He tells Hamm it is not time for his painkiller; and when it is time, he declares there is none. If Clov's "cruelty" would mitigate Hamm's in a conventional play, Hamm's parents' initial cruelty would explain it. When Hamm, as an infant, had cried, his parents had simply moved out of earshot. But there is no occasion for either mitigation or etiology. For there is one consideration, omnipresent in the speeches and silences of the play, that acquits all of its characters. Their petty cruelties count for nothing against the cruelty of their condition: existence, which has decreed a gradual loss of all power, while the increasingly impotent man either fails to adjust and reaps suffering or adjusts and reaps boredom.[7] The degrees of cruelty between one man and another are a tiny differential

[7] The terms are again from Beckett's monograph on Proust, p. 18.

against the cruelty of what they face; the hardness of their hearts is silly-putty against the hardness of the wall they are up against. "You're on earth," Hamm cries out to the suppliant in the "chronicle" he is devising. "There's no cure for that."

The discussion of Hamm's cruelty could be extended to any other character or any trait which the auditor attempts to pin on that character. Is Nell really "sentimental"? It is she who shocks Nagg by suggesting that "nothing is funnier than unhappiness"—hardly a sentimental view. Are the characters really like the personifications in mystery plays or *autos sacramentales,* as Martin Esslin suggests,[8] when it is difficult to make character traits stick to them let alone frozen attributes of moral identity. Are they indeed characters as we understand the fictive personage—possessed of traits of varying "organization" or strength, changing with time and event, possessed of a will, character, and temperament? Susan Sontag has written in an article on Godard that his film technique tends to "consume" points of view.[9] Does not Beckett's technique consume character? One is teased out of thought about their individual make-up or archetypal destiny. One waits to see how they will move, be moved, with what invention they will deck the vacuum they inhabit, with what grace they will bear their agony, how cunningly they will play a game they must lose.

If Beckett's characters change our notion of character, force us to temporarily put away our techniques and labels of character analysis, his plays force us to modify our notion of the drama. There is no rising action, falling action, for all is fallen at the play's opening. There is no linear movement—the first tableau is the last one, except that Clov is at the end dressed for a trip he may or may not take. Indeed, the fact that we begin and end with tableaux, that no events fall between them, that there has not been a change of heart, mind, situation, venue, that we are no closer to a reasoned grasp on the characters' natures or the meaning of what they enact, makes us wonder if it is truly a drama we are looking at—a work that unfolds in time as well as space. As the language becomes less discursive and more incantatory, a much remarked quality of the play, do we not feel that we are in the presence of a linguistic art form that nevertheless suggests the properties of non-linguistic forms—painting, music? It is true that *Endgame* requires ninety minutes of playing time, that its speeches are arranged sequentially and assigned to four players. One wonders, nevertheless, what an art critic (or a gifted amateur art critic like Beckett himself) might see in it. Might he not capture its special quality for us if he regards

[8] *The Theatre of the Absurd* (New York, 1961), p. 39.

[9] *Partisan Review* (Spring, 1968), p. 297.

it as a presentational form[10] enjoining him to describe what he sees rather than analyzing it, discover how it may have been made rather than how it satisfies the demands of a pre-existent form?

Until such a critic appears, one can only fail as best one can to describe that quality, to catch it, and to marvel. To marvel at a play that for all "the fetid odor of human suffering" [11] it exudes is informed by a strange gaiety.[12] To marvel at a work that contains vulgar joking ("Peace to our arses") alongside genuine lyricism ("You cried for night; it falls; now cry in darkness" or "Old endgame lost of old, play and lose and have done with losing") without a moment's failure of harmony. To marvel at a nightmare in which the Freudian principles of condensation and displacement have given over to the Aristotelian unities of time and place. To marvel at a game during which the point now goes to Hamm, now to Clov, yet when the final tableau is struck, the score remains resolutely at zero.

[10] The term is Suzanne Langer's. "In the non-discursive mode that speaks directly to sense, however, there is no intrinsic generality. It is first and foremost a direct *presentation* of an individual object." *Philosophy in a New Key,* 3rd ed. (Cambridge, 1960), p. 96.

[11] This characterization of the play's ambiance is Pronko's, p. 46. See above, fn. 3.

[12] Mike Nichols, the director, stated in a *New York Times* Sunday drama section interview that he should like to stage *Endgame* in order to bring out its comic element. January 23, 1966, p. 7.

Endgame

by Ruby Cohn

Or pondering Christ's
parthian shaft:
It is finished.
Murphy

When he translated *Fin de Partie* into *Endgame,* Beckett classified it as a "play." [1] Johan Huizinga defines play as "an activity which proceeds within certain limits of time and space, in a visible order, according to rules freely accepted, and outside the sphere of necessity or material utility." [2] In *Godot,* the tramps invent games to play while they wait for Godot to come. In *Endgame* there is no longer a hope that anyone may come; games are at an end, and nobody feels like playing. Yet the show goes on.

In *Endgame* the physical situation on stage is instantly grimmer than that of *Godot.* From the country road suggesting far-off space, and the tree connoting growth, we move to a dim room whose two high, tiny windows, facing earth and sea, respectively, are curtained; the lone picture has its face to the wall. Egress from the room is possible only to

---

"Endgame." *From* Samuel Beckett: The Comic Gamut *by Ruby Cohn (New Brunswick, New Jersey: Rutgers University Press, 1962), pp. 226–42. Reprinted by permission of Rutgers University Press.*

[1] Jean-Jacques Mayoux, "Le Théâtre de Samuel Beckett, *Etudes Anglaises* (October, 1957), 350n, quotes a letter from Beckett to him: "La rédaction définitive de *Fin de Partie* est de 56. Main J'avais abordé ce travail bien avant, peut-être en 54. Une première puis une seconde version en deux actes ont précédé celle en un acte que vous connaissez."

In spite of the success of *Godot,* Roger Blin was unable to find a Paris theatre manager who would risk producing the grimmer *Fin de Partie,* and the first production (in French) therefore took place at the Royal Court Theatre in London on April 3, 1957. The French publication by Editions de Minuit appeared a month later, and Beckett's English translation, *Endgame,* was published by Grove Press in 1958.

[2] Huizinga, *A Study of the Play Element in Culture* (Boston, 1955), p. 132.

Clov—and not to Hamm in his armchair on castors, not to Nagg and Nell in their respective ash bins. Much of the comic stage business revolves around this circumscribed physical situation: Clov covers and uncovers the ash bin dwellers, and they themselves pop into sight and disappear. Clov climbs on a ladder to see out of the two windows; he wheels Hamm around the room and returns him to place; Hamm insists upon being first "right in" and then "more or less in" the center.

The plot of *Endgame,* like that of *Godot,* can be more easily summarized than can Beckett's later fiction. But relationships are ambiguous, and interpretation complex. Nagg and Nell are Hamm's parents, but Clov is variously called his son, menial, creature, and dog. An offstage Mother Pegg is never revealed as the mother of anybody, and like the rest of the off-stage world, she is presumably dead when the play begins. After Clov sights a small boy on the beach, he prepares to leave Hamm. The small boy, however, does not appear on scene, and Hamm, covering his face with the bloody handkerchief of the opening tableau, seems resigned to the death that has already overtaken—perhaps at his instigation—the remaining world.

The plot is nakedly built on cruelty, suffering, and death. Beckett himself describes *Endgame*: "Rather difficult and elliptic, mostly depending on the power of the text to claw, more inhuman than Godot." [3] One analysis of *Endgame* reads it as a tragedy, but a tragedy that vacillates between terror and farce.[4] In *Godot,* Vladimir complains that it hurts to laugh, but in *Endgame* Hamm and Clov reiterate that they no longer feel like laughing. Nevertheless, Clov's five brief laughs are the first sounds in *Endgame,* and the play may be interpreted as a bitterly ironic version of creation and resurrection, making incidental use of comic devices, above all repetition.

"It is finished"—the last words of Christ on the Cross, according to the Gospel of St. John—are echoed in the first words of the English version of *Endgame*—Clov's "Finished, it's finished, nearly finished, it must be nearly finished." In Hamm's first speech, he twice declares, "It's time it ended." Shortly afterwards, when Clov wishes to withdraw from Hamm to look at his kitchen wall, Hamm sneers, "The wall! And what do you see on your wall? Mene, mene." The prophet Daniel translated *Mene* as "God hath numbered thy kingdom, and finished it" (5:26).

After Hamm's father, Nagg, tells a joke in which a pair of tailor-made trousers is exalted above God's created world, Hamm cries out, "Have you not finished? Will you never finish? Will this never finish?"

[3] *Village Voice,* March 19, 1958, pp. 8, 15.

[4] Richard Eastman, "The Strategy of Samuel Beckett's *Endgame,*" *Modern Drama* (May, 1959), 36–44.

Midway through the play, in one of the many duets between Hamm and Clov, Hamm pleads, "Why don't you finish us? (*Pause.*) I'll tell you the combination of the cupboard if you promise to finish me." Clov replies, "I couldn't finish you." Hamm shrugs, "Then you won't finish me." Several times, Clov repeats that the toy dog he is creating for Hamm "isn't finished." Just before Hamm embarks on his own artistic creation, he almost echoes Clov's opening phrases, "It's finished, we're finished. (*Pause.*) Nearly finished."

As the comic and intolerable emphasis on waiting summarizes the major action of *Godot,* so the many "finished's" point to the death of a world in *Endgame*. "Outside of here it's death," warns Hamm, and in the play we watch death's relentless invasion of "here." The verbal music of *Endgame* has a dying fall; the constant repetition yields macabre mirth.

There are, successively, incongruously, repetitively, "no more" bicycle wheels, pap, nature, sugarplums, tides, rugs, pain-killer, and, finally, coffins. Clov kills a flea on stage and seeks to kill a rat off stage. Nell dies on stage, Nagg no longer answers from his ash bin, Hamm and Clov both remain *"motionless"* at the final curtain. The dramatic action presents the death of the stock props of Western civilization—family cohesion, filial devotion, parental and connubial love, faith in God, empirical knowledge, and artistic creation.

With characteristic irony, Beckett accents the cruel inhumanity of *Endgame* by frequent evocation of the Bible in the light of its delineation of man's role, particularly with respect to the superhuman. Thus, Hamm, son of Nagg, instantly recalls Ham, son of Noah. Nagg, like Noah, has fathered the remnant of humanity, but rather than make a covenant with God, he tells a joke at God's expense. Biblical Noah faithfully follows God's command to perpetuate all species by thriftily introducing couples into the ark; but Beckett's Nagg is indifferent to, or unaware of, the universal death outside the shelter.

Although Noah's animals are absent from *Endgame,* the play abounds in animal associations: Hamm is an edible part of pig, and Clov either its spice accompaniment, or perhaps a reference to the cloven-hoofed animals which, pigs excepted, were the only permissible meat for biblical Jews. A nag is a small horse, and Nell a common name for a horse; Nagg-nag and Nell-knell are puns as well. Hamm refers to Clov as his dog, and Clov makes a toy dog for Hamm. Clov feeds Nagg Spratt's medium animal biscuits. An off-stage rat and an on-stage flea are objects of Clov's murderous intent, for rather than propagate all species, Nagg's progeny, Hamm and (perhaps) Clov, seek to extinguish them. The flea in Clov's trousers is fiercely and farcically destroyed lest a new evolutionary line lead to humanity again. Even a punning sex joke is made to serve the theme of universal destruction. After applying insecticide freely, with exaggerated, slapstick gestures, Clov adjusts his trousers. He has killed the flea "unless he's laying doggo."

> *Hamm.* Laying! Lying, you mean. Unless he's *lying* doggo.
>
> *Clov.* Ah? One says lying? One doesn't say laying?
>
> *Hamm.* Use your head, can't you. If he was laying we'd be bitched. (Grove Press, 34)

In Genesis, "Ham, the father of Canaan, saw the nakedness of his father, and told his two brethren without" (9:22). Beckett's Hamm, by ironic contrast, has no brethren and cannot see; his Canaan is circumscribed to the "bare interior" of the room on the stage, and his father is relegated to an ash bin in that room. Biblical Noah curses his son for seeing him naked, and Beckett's Hamm curses his father for conceiving him. The biblical curse of Noah to Ham is: "a servant of servants shall he be unto his brethren" (9:25). Nagg also curses his son, but not with a prophecy of servitude, for Hamm is master of his domain, which is reduced to the stage room.

Hamm refers to his kingdom—an ironic name for the room before our eyes. In production, his armchair looks like a mock-throne, his toque like a mock-crown. He utters high-handed orders to Clov, a servant who is intermittently good and faithful. Both Hamm and Clov suggest that the world off stage perished by Hamm's will. Even more cruel than Hamm's own lust for destruction is that of the "I" of Hamm's story, which, like the play proper, is full of biblical reminders.

Hamm sets his chronicle on Christmas Eve, that time of birth rather than death, of peace on earth, and good will towards men. But Hamm, ironically, fills the narrator-protagonist of his tale with ill will in a desolate world, which Hamm describes in terms of numbers on thermometer, heliometer, anemometer, and hygrometer. Just as Hamm is lord of a lifeless earth, and sole custodian of its dwindling supplies, so Hamm's narrator-hero rules a similar domain. The father of a starving child crawls before him, begging for food. With charity towards none, but cruelly recalling a divine charity towards a people in exile, Hamm's "I" screams at the groveling father, "But what in God's name do you imagine? . . . That there's manna in heaven still for imbeciles like you?"

Similarly, the blindness, darkness, suffering, and above all death that fill *Endgame* comment ironically on a biblical context. The most frequently repeated line of the play is Hamm's "Is it not time for my pain-killer?" Although Hamm is literally asking Clov for a pill, it becomes increasingly evident that the only true pain-killer is death. When Clov asks Hamm whether he believes in the life to come, the sardonic answer is, "Mine was always that." The ring of the alarm clock is "Fit to wake the dead!"

On two separate occasions, Hamm cries out in anguish, "Father, Father!" and, as Jean-Jacques Mayoux has suggested, "How can we not think of the 'Eli Eli' of that other supreme moment?" [5] Towards the end of the play, Hamm utters several phrases which derisively twist Scripture: "Get out of here and love one another! Lick your neighbor as yourself! . . . The end is in the beginning. . . . Good. . . . Good. . . . Peace to our—arses." In the French text Hamm compares the small boy outside the shelter to a dying Moses gazing at the Promised Land.

Since *Endgame* is unmistakably a play about an end of a world, there are many recollections of the Book of Revelations. In the vision of St. John the Divine, Christ says he has "the keys of hell and of death," in ironic contrast to Hamm, who knows the combination of a cupboard that presumably contains the wherewithal to keep them *alive* in their hell in the shelter.

Revelations is full of phrases about light and darkness, sea and earth, beginning and end, life and death. After the destruction of Babylon, a great voice from heaven utters the words, "It is done." In the New Jerusalem, "The length and the breadth and the height of it are equal," even as the length, breadth, and height of Clov's kitchen, whose thousand cubic feet might be a caricature reminder of the millennium of Revelations.

Within the tight text of *Endgame,* the frequency and mockery of the biblical echoes cannot be ignored in any interpretation of the play, and the fourth Gospel is crucial for such interpretation. Not only does the English *Endgame* contain the fugal variations upon Christ's last words, "It is finished," but in this gospel particularly, Christ affirms that He is the light; He speaks of "my Father" and "my Father's house." Beckett's Hamm has dispensed and extinguished light; he calls upon his father and insists that his house is the only asylum.

St. John tells the story of Lazarus, resurrected by Christ, and we learn both from that account and the Passion that in biblical times corpses were wrapped in linen clothes, a napkin around the head, and anointed with oil and spices. In *Endgame,* Clov may be a spice anointing corpses; it is he who lifts the sheets from near-corpses, but it is Hamm who focuses attention on the napkin that covers his head when the play opens and closes—even as a napkin covered the head of Lazarus and of Christ.

In the productions of *Endgame,* Clov opens the play by drawing the

[5] "The Theatre of Samuel Beckett," *Perspective* (Autumn, 1959), 149.

curtains at the two windows, and removing the sheets from the ash bins and Hamm's armchair. These gestures are performed like a ritual, or a mock-ritual. Hamm's first gestures, too, are formal—his slow lifting of the blood-stained handkerchief from his face; his meticulous wiping of eyes, face, and the dark glasses that hide his sightless eyes; his methodical folding of the handkerchief before placing it elegantly in the breast pocket of his dressing gown. Just before the final curtain, Hamm removes the handkerchief from the breast pocket over his heart, and it is seen to be stained with blood so as to suggest human features. He finally covers his head, where he previously heard his heart dripping.

Only in St. John's Gospel does doubting Thomas say, after the crucifixion: "Except I shall see in his hands the print of the nails, and put my finger into the print of the nails, and thrust my hand into his side, I will not believe." Jesus then appears to Thomas, who then believes, and Jesus admonishes: "Thomas, because thou hast seen me, thou hast believed: blessed are they that have not seen, and yet have believed."

In *Endgame,* there are apparently no believers—neither those who see (however dimly) nor blind Hamm. The onstage prayer, which Beckett refused to change upon request of the London censor, goes unanswered. The nails leave no print, or their print is perhaps no longer evidence for belief. Several critics have pointed out that Clov is *clou* is *"nail,"* that Nell and Nagg derive from Germanic *naegel,* meaning "nail." [6] To these might be added the offstage Mother Pegg, for a "peg" is also a nail. Latin *hamus* is hook, a kind of crooked nail, so that Hamm may be viewed as another nail. In this sense, every proper name in *Endgame* is a nail, and "nailhood" seems sardonically to symbolize humanity, whose role is to nail Christ to the Cross. All the characters are thus instruments working towards the play's paradoxical opening word, "Finished."

But Hamm is also contained in "hammer," which strikes at nails, and is thus an even more active agent in the crucifying. If Hamm is a Christ figure, he is also a crucifier.

Hamm as biblical *Ham,* as Latin *hamus,* as contained in "hammer," indicates a revival of Becket's early taste for puns.[7] The twisted quotation of *Murphy,* "In the beginning was the pun," parodies the opening sentence of the Gospel of St. John: "In the beginning was the Word, and the Word was with God, and the Word was God."

[6] E.g., Thomas Barvour, "Beckett and Ionesco," *Husdon Review* (Summer, 1958), 271–75.

[7] The most pyrotechnic display of paronomasia in *Endgame* is Beckett's translation of Nagg's multipunning joke from French (36–38) to English (22–23).

In *Endgame,* words serve to form not only puns but jokes, prayers, proverbs, prophecies, maledictions, chronicles, poems, and, of course, the dialogue of the play. (Joyce called words "quashed quotatoes, messes of mottage.") Clov accuses Hamm, the wielder of words, "I use the words you taught me. If they don't mean anything any more, teach me others." Near the end, Clov complains, "They [the words that remain] have nothing to say."

For all their combination into various minor genres, there is an astonishing stinginess in the number of words Beckett allows himself in *Endgame*. Again and again, we find the same words repeated, the same words issuing from different mouths. In spite of his extraordinary vocabulary and impressive command of several languages, Beckett deliberately limits the words of *Endgame,* charging each word with an enormous burden.

"Why this farce day after day?" ask both Nell and Clov. Both exclaim nostalgically, "Once!" Nell is still able to sigh lyrically (twice), "Ah yesterday," but Clov defines yesterday as "that bloody awful day, long ago, before this bloody awful day." Time and weather are both "the same as usual." Hamm, obsessed with himself, still continues to question Clov, "How are your eyes? How are your legs?" and Nagg, "How are your stumps?" "The bastard!" exclaims Clov about his flea, and Hamm about God. Several times, Clov repeats to Hamm, and Nell to Nagg, "I'll leave you." Several times, Clov repeats to Hamm, "Something is taking its course," and Hamm retorts at last, "I'm taking my course." Even scenic directions are constantly repeated; in French *"même jeu"* virtually summarizes the action of the play. Many statements are repeated, prefaced by a "then" of resignation. Whole dialogues are built comically around a few words, as in the following example:

Clov. So you all want me to leave you.
Hamm. Naturally.
Clov. Then I'll leave you.
Hamm. You can't leave us.
Clov. Then I won't leave you. (*Pause.*)
Hamm. Why don't you finish us? (*Pause.*) I'll tell you the combination of the cupboard if you promise to finish me.
Clov. I couldn't finish you.
Hamm. Then you won't finish me.
Clov. I'll leave you, I have things to do. (37)

In no other drama is the quantity of words so drastically reduced, mocking St. John's Words that are both with God, and God. Nevertheless, St. John's opening sentence states Beckett's fundamental and recurrent theme, and nowhere so ironically and yet so desperately as in *Endgame.* The seemingly disparate elements of the play—the end of a world, biblical fathers and sons, masters and servants, ritual and crucifixion, word and Word—do finally cohere. But the line of coherence will be more apparent if it is traced through several earlier Beckett works.

On the occasion of Joyce's fiftieth birthday, in 1934, Beckett published an acrostic poem of homage to the older Irish writer. The title "Home Olga," is a pun on *Homo Logos,* Word-Man.

J might be made sit up for a jade of hope (and exile, don't you know)
A nd Jesus and Jesuits juggernauted in the haemorrhoidal isle,
M odo et forma anal maiden giggling to death in stomacho.
E for the erythrite of love and silence and the sweet noo style,
S woops and loops of love and silence in the eye of the sun and view of the mew,

J uvante Jah and a Jain or two and the tip of a friendly yiddophile.
O for an opal of faith and cunning winking adieu, adieu, adieu;
Y esterday shall be tomorrow, riddle me that my rapparee;
C he sarà sarà che fu, that's more than Homer knows how to spew,
E xempli gratia: ecce himself and the pickthank agnus—e.o.o.e.[8]

In the last lines, Christ and Joyce are coupled, if not confused, as examples of word-men, by whom "yesterday shall be tomorrow." The implication is of a Viconian, cyclical resurrection, presumably through the Logos that tells tales (pickthank). Joyce himself viewed reality as a paradigm, and he conceived the function of the artist-maker as an obligation to recognize coincidences in time, space, and significance—a coincidence frequently compressed in the pun.

In his unpublished play, *Eleutheria,* Beckett puns on Olga and Logos. The vaguely authorial hero, Victor Krap, is engaged to the beautiful Olga Skunk. At the end of the play, hero and heroine do not marry, and, as might be expected in a Beckett work, they probably live *un*happily ever after. Beckett can see no Victor-y in the Logos, and the two characters go their respective crappy and stinking ways.

In French, Logos is usually translated by *Verbe,* not by *parole* or *mot.* In the tight prose of *L'Innommable,* the last volume of his trilogy, Beckett slips a *verbe* of biblical resonance among his torrents of *mots* into his indictment of *la parole:* "je suis tous ces mots, tous ces étrangers, cette poussière de verbe." In the second *Texte pour rien,* Beckett puns, "Les mots aussi, lents, lents, le sujet meurt avant d'atteindre le verbe, les mots s'arrêtent aussi." Literally, the subject

[8] *Contempo* (February 2, 1934), 3.

dies before reaching the verb, but more significantly, all subjects die before being embodied in the Word.

No puns on *Verbe* or Logos appear in *Endgame,* but in the opening chapter of the Gospel of St. John, it is also written that "the Word was made flesh," and the grossest, most palpable flesh is the mammalian ham. Hamm of *Endgame* is the word made flesh, while still retaining his control over the word. Like Christ, like Joyce, Hamm is a Word-Man.

By name and dialogue, Hamm is further linked to another word-man, Shakespeare, who is described by Coleridge in almost Beckettian terms—"the great ever living dead man." Hamm, as most critics have noted, is a ham-actor, and contains at least that aspect of Hamlet. Hamm has also been compared to Prospero, and in the English text of *Endgame,* Beckett makes the parallel explicit. When Hamm has told his father his story, and betrayed his promise of a sugarplum, when Nagg, no longer able to rouse Nell, retires into his own ash bin, Hamm summarizes his situation in French, "Finie la rigolade." But the slang is not translated into English; Beckett renders the lines as, "Our revels now are ended."

The words, of course, are Prospero's from Act IV of *The Tempest,* and they are surely introduced to underline the striking parallels and ironic contrasts between the two plays. Prospero's entire speech is apposite:

> Our revels now are ended. These our actors,
> As I foretold you, were all spirits and
> Are melted into air, into thin air;
> And, like the baseless fabric of this vision,
> The cloud-capp'd towers, the gorgeous palaces,
> The solemn temples, the great globe itself,
> Yea, all which it inherit, shall dissolve,
> And, like this insubstantial pageant faded,
> Leave not a rack behind. We are such stuff
> As dreams are made on, and our little life
> Is rounded with a sleep.

Shakespeare's towers, palaces, and temples are absent from the "bare interior" of Beckett's stage, which may literally represent that container of dreams (or nightmares)—the human skull.[9] If so, each window is an eye, Shakespeare's "great globe" appearing grayly through the one, and his "multitudinous seas" as grayly through the other. All

[9] Roger Blin's set, in the French production supervised by Beckett, was vaguely oval. The interior of a skull, owner unknown, is a recurrent locale in Beckett's fiction.

who inherit or inhabit the globe are reduced to four in *Endgame,* two in their nightcaps in ash bins, one immoblized in his dressing gown, and the fourth shrunken and unable to sit. The sleep that rounds their little life is deepened to the death that pervades the atmosphere of *Endgame* from its opening lines.

By Act V of *The Tempest,* Shakespeare returns to comedy, where, by Renaissance decorum, death has no dominion. Prospero breaks his staff, drowns his book, rewards the innocent, and pardons the guilty. While waiting for him, Ferdinand and Miranda are shown playing chess.

In both French and English, *Fin de Partie* and *Endgame* refer to the third and final phase of a chess game.[10] Chess is, of course, a game, a form of play, as is a work of art. Hamm's opening line, "Me to play," is emphasized by the wrenching of normal English word order (in French by the desperation of "à moi"). Like Hamlet, Hamm is responsible for a play within the play—his chronicle. But even in the direct action of *Endgame,* there are constant comic references to the play as a play.

Near the beginning, Hamm comments, "The thing is impossible." Somewhat later, "This is slow work." Several times, he encourages himself, "We're getting on." After a while, "This is not much fun." Hamm's "This is deadly," spoken while Clov is offstage, is the cue for Clov's ironic comment on the action, "Things are livening up. (*He gets up on ladder, raises the telescope, lets it fall.*) I did it on purpose. (*He gets down, picks up the telescope, turns it on auditorium.*) I see . . . a multitude . . . in transports . . . of joy. (*Pause.*) That's what I call a magnifier" (29).

As the end approaches, the references to the play as a play are more numerous and pointed. When Hamm declares that Clov can't leave him, Clov asks, "What is there to keep me here?" Hamm retorts, "The dialogue." A little later, Hamm reiterates, "Me to play," holds his handkerchief before him, repeats, "We're getting on," and folds the handkerchief back in his pocket.

Close to the end, Clov implores Hamm to stop playing, but he replies, "Never!" Hamm informs Clov angrily that he is uttering an "aside," then that he is "warming up for [his] last soliloquy." When the small boy is sighted through the window, Hamm hopes that it is "not an underplot." Abandoned by Clov—"This is what we call making an exit"—Hamm utters his final "Me to play," and reveals that from the beginning he was destined to lose, "Old endgame lost

[10] For fuller discussion of chess in *Endgame,* see Eastman, "The Strategy of Beckett's *Endgame*"; Vivian Mercier, "How to Read *Endgame,*" *Griffin* (June, 1959), 10–14.

of old, play and lose and have done with losing." His exclamations of "Discard . . . Deuce" recall a card game, and further extend the generalization of play.[11] So, too, the whistle with which Hamm can no longer summon Clov has an important role in various games. The futile gesture of blind Hamm wiping his glasses, in the end as at the beginning of *Endgame,* suggests the gratuitous quality of all play, including art.

In his last lines, Hamm haltingly quotes Baudelaire,[12] then briefly continues his own chronicle. Crying out to his father for the last time, throwing away his toy dog and the whistle, crying out to Clov for the last time and hearing no answer, Hamm prepares for his end: "Since that's the way we're playing it, let's play it that way, and speak no more about it, speak no more." Although his final words are addressed to the blood-stained handkerchief, this penultimate sentence reflects ironically upon a game of words, which leads only to silence.

The last move of Hamm's game is to cover his face with the blood-stained handkerchief of the opening tableau. The recollection is of St. Veronica's handkerchief stamped with Christ's features (already used in earlier Beckett works). The suggestion is that Hamm's life is a Passion, also consummated at Golgotha, the place of a skull. But if Hamm's death closes the play, is there a resurrection?

Perhaps *Endgame,* with characteristic Beckett ambivalence, implies two resurrections—one occurring just after the curtain rises, and one just after it finally falls. As has been mentioned, the opening action, silent except for five brief laughs (possibly recalling Christ's five wounds?), is performed like a mock-ritual. Sheets are removed from inert objects, and three people come to life—slowly and feebly—on the stage. The opening word is Clov's paradoxical "Finished," but his phrases trail off in some doubt. Hamm, the word-man made flesh, is "getting on" in years. He is blind and can therefore not rely on knowledge through perception. He has relegated his parents—both their teachings and tenderness—to ash bins and nightcaps.

Far, far in the past are those days when his parents rode through France and Italy on a tandem, when Hamm himself manipulated a bicycle, when Clov pleaded for a bicycle and rode a horse, when body was in efficient union with mind, and man and his carrier could complement each other.[13] By the time of *Endgame,* the delights of the body are grotesque anachronisms. Nagg and Nell laugh uproariously at the accident in which they lost their legs. Keats's line, "Bold lover,

[11] Charles Shattuck of the University of Illinois suggested this point to me.

[12] Leonard Pronko of Pomona College called the Baudelaire line to my attention.

[13] For fuller discussion of Beckett's bicycles, see Hugh Kenner, "The Cartesian Centaur," *Perspective* (Autumn, 1959), 132–41.

never, never, canst thou kiss," is hideously if hilariously caricatured when Nagg and Nell strain towards each other from their respective ash bins, their "very white" faces like death masks. Beauty is dead, truth is dead, happiness a subject for farce. "Nothing is funnier than unhappiness," Nell sets the tone of *Endgame*. Once born, or resurrected, or merely set in motion, Hamm reluctantly yet compulsively forces the show to go on.

Paralyzed himself, he directs the action, even as a director does a play, even as God perhaps directs the world. The infinitesimal movements of his armchair, human life and death—all are subject to Hamm's commands, as long as he is in command. And yet, his activities are ridiculously restricted to composing a chronicle, to praying half-heartedly when he runs out of characters, and above all to giving orders to Clov, variously designated as his dog, menial, creature, and son.

Early in the play, Hamm makes a prophecy about Clov, and we recall other blind prophets—Tiresias, Oedipus, Samson.[14] Hamm's prophecy ends, "Infinite emptiness will be all around you, all the resurrected dead of all the ages wouldn't fill it, and there you'll be like a little bit of grit in the middle of the steppe. (*Pause.*) Yes, one day you'll know what it is, *you'll be like me,* except that you won't have anyone with you, because you won't have had pity on anyone and because there won't be anyone to have pity on" (my italics).

Ironic as the word "pity" sounds in Hamm's mouth, there is someone for Clov to pity, once the small boy is sighted. This little child—real or imagined—is the cue for Hamm to dismiss Clov: "I don't need you any more." Perhaps the small boy will take Clov's place as Hamm's servant, while Clov goes out to die in the desert. If, after the final curtain, Hamm is resurrected, the small boy would remove the sheets in the opening ritual, and Hamm, uncovering his face, would replay his part as hero-victim-director-actor-author. The pattern of such a resurrection would be circular.

Although Clov is the past tense of "cleave," he remains present to the final curtain. Beckett is rumored to have remarked that in *Godot,* the audience wonders whether Godot will ever come, and in *Endgame* they wonder whether Clov will ever leave. It is evident that Beckett intends the wonder in both cases, up to and beyond the end of the plays.

While the audience wonders, blind Hamm understands that he has been abandoned, and he proceeds to make himself absolute for death. In the closing scene, *"He covers his face with handkerchief, lowers his arms to armrests, remains motionless."* If this immobility is death, and

[14] In *Godot,* blind Pozzo of Act II denies the prophetic powers of the blind.

if, after the final curtain, Clov does leave the shelter, perhaps he goes only far enough to fetch the boy, so as to make of him a dog, a menial, a creature, and a son. Perhaps Clov will discover a combination to another cupboard, or perhaps he and the boy, according to some principle of parsimony, will live on leftovers in Clov's millennial kitchen. Then Clov would fulfill Hamm's prophecy with a vengeance; he would not only be like Hamm, he would *be* Hamm, word made flesh, instead of its trivial spice accompaniment. The play, perhaps on a reduced stage, perhaps in a reduced skull, would be replayed with Clov as Hamm. The pattern of such a resurrection would be cyclical.

Already, Clov at the beginning of *Endgame* has shrunk to where he needs a ladder to see out of the window (eye?) of the stage (skull?). It is Clov whose opening line echoes Christ's last words. Like Christ, he speaks of a father and his father's home. In some productions, he stands behind Hamm's chair with arms outstretched as though crucified. Once, Clov implies that "it" can end only if he sings. In his last long speech, Clov shifts from "*They* said to me" to "*I* say to myself" (my italics). Dressed though he is at the last for sun or rain, he does not actually leave the "bare interior," which is a shelter from all weathers. In the French text, Hamm's comment on Clov's discovery of the small boy is "La pierre levée"—the sign of Christ's resurrection. Clov may have invented the small boy who will serve as Clov, even as Clov may have been the small boy in Hamm's literary invention.

In all Beckett's later works, there is no way of distinguishing fact from fiction. Their inseparability and irreconcilability is a recurrent theme of his trilogy of novels. In each successive novel, the hero-narrator undergoes further physical degeneration. Ironically, composition takes place during decomposition. Just as dying had a sexual connotation for the Elizabethans, so it seems to have a creative one for Beckett—artistically creative.

The verbal spareness of *Endgame* is a startling contrast to the unparagraphed verbal rush of the trilogy, but in both works the heroes are word-men, and in both works one word-man is replaceable and (perhaps) replaced by another. In *Endgame,* Clov, Hamm, and Nagg—three generations—are also three stages of physical decomposition. Like Malone in the trilogy, it is Hamm, the middle member, who is at the height (such as it is) of his creative powers. But as the focus of *Endgame* narrows to the Hamm-Clov relationship, the tension is tautened between creator and creature until, finally, after the end of the play as played, one is (perhaps) replaced by the other, and the whole absurd, heartbreaking cycle begins again. Resurrection into another and reduced life, into another and slower death, may take place—if at all—only through the play of creation.

Life in the Box

by Hugh Kenner

. . . [T]he stage is a place to wait. The place itself waits, when no one is in it. When the curtain rises on *Endgame,* sheets drape all visible objects as in a furniture warehouse. Clov's first act is to uncurtain the two high windows and inspect the universe; his second is to remove the sheets and fold them carefully over his arm, disclosing two ash cans and a figure in an armchair. This is so plainly a metaphor for waking up that we fancy the stage, with its high peepholes, to be the inside of an immense skull. It is also a ritual for starting the play; Yeats arranged such a ritual for *At the Hawk's Well,* and specified a black cloth and a symbolic song. It is finally a removal from symbolic storage of the objects that will be needed during the course of the performance. When the theatre is empty it is sensible to keep them covered against dust. So we are reminded at the outset that what we are to witness is a dusty dramatic exhibition, repeated and repeatable. The necessary objects include three additional players (two of them in ash cans). Since none of them will move from his station we can think of them after the performance as being kept permanently on stage, and covered with their dust cloths again until tomorrow night.

The rising of the curtain disclosed these sheeted forms; the removal of the sheets disclosed the protagonist and his ash cans; the next stage is for the protagonist to uncover his own face, which he does with a yawn, culminating this three-phase strip tease with the revelation of a very red face and black glasses. His name, we gather from the program, is Hamm, a name for an actor. He is also Hamlet, bounded in a nutshell, fancying himself king of infinite space, but troubled by bad dreams; he is also "a toppled Prospero," [1] remarking partway through

---

From "Life in the Box." From Samuel Beckett: A Critical Study *by Hugh Kenner (New York: Grove Press, 1961; London: Calder & Boyars Ltd., 1962), pp. 155–65.*

[1] This admirable phrase is Mr. Roy Walker's, in the December 1958 *Twentieth Century.*

the play, with judicious pedantry, "our revels now are ended"; he is also the Hammer to which Clov, Nagg and Nell (Fr. *clou,* Ger. *Nagel,* Eng. *nail*) stand in passive relationship; by extension, a chess player ("Me—[*he yawns*]—to play"); but also (since Clov must wheel him about) himself a chessman, probably the imperiled King.

Nagg and Nell in their dustbins appear to be pawns; Clov, with his arbitrarily restricted movements ("I can't sit.") and his equestrian background ("And your rounds? Always on foot?" "Sometimes on horse.") resembles the Knight, and his perfectly cubical kitchen ("ten feet by ten feet by ten feet, nice dimensions, nice proportions") resembles a square on the chessboard translated into three dimensions. He moves back and forth, into it and out of it, coming to the succor of Hamm and then retreating. At the endgame's end the pawns are forever immobile and Clov is poised for a last departure from the board, the status quo forever menaced by an expected piece glimpsed through the window, and King Hamm abandoned in check:

> Old endgame lost of old, play and lose and have done with losing. . . . Since that's the way we're playing it, let's play it that way . . . and speak no more about it . . . speak no more.

Even if we had not the information that the author of this work has been known to spend hours playing chess with himself (a game at which you always lose[2]), we should have been alerted to his long-standing interest in its strategy by the eleventh chapter of *Murphy,* where Murphy's first move against Mr. Endon, the standard P—K_4, is described as "the primary cause of all [his] subsequent difficulties." (The same might be said of getting born, an equally conventional opening.) Chess has several peculiarities which lend themselves to the metaphors of this jagged play. It is a game of leverage, in which the significance of a move may be out of all proportion to the local disturbance it effects ("A flea! This is awful! What a day!"). It is a game of silences, in which new situations are appraised: hence Beckett's most frequent stage direction, *"Pause."* It is a game of steady attrition; by the time we reach the endgame the board is nearly bare, as bare as Hamm's world where there are no more bicycle wheels, sugarplums, pain killers, or coffins, let alone people. And it is a game which by the successive removal of screening pieces constantly extends the range of lethal forces, until at the endgame peril from a key piece sweeps down whole ranks and files. The king is hobbled by the rule which allows him to move in any direction but only one square at a time; Hamm's circuit of the stage and return to center perhaps exhibits him patrolling the

[2] Or always win. "One of the thieves was saved. It's a reasonable percentage."

inner boundaries of the little nine-square territory he commands. To venture further will evidently expose him to check. ("Outside of here it's death.") His knight shuttles to and fro, his pawns are pinned. No threat is anticipated from the auditorium, which is presumably off the board; and a periodic reconnaissance downfield through the windows discloses nothing but desolation until very near the end. But on his last inspection of the field Clov is dismayed. Here the English text is inexplicably sketchy; in the French one we have,

Clov. Aïeaïeaïe!
Hamm. C'est une feuille? Une fleur? Une toma—(*il bâille*)—te?
Clov. (*regardant*) Je t'en foutrai des tomates! Quelqu'un! C'est quelqu'un!
Hamm. Eh bien, va l'exterminer. (*Clov descend de l'escabeau.*) Quelqu'un! (*Vibrant.*) Fais ton devoir!

[*Clov.* Aïeaïeaïe!
Hamm. It's a leaf? A flower? A toma—(*he yawns*)—to?
Clov (*looking*). Damn the tomatoes! Someone! It's someone!
Hamm. Well, go exterminate him. (*Clove gets down from the stool.*) Someone! (*With trembling voice.*) Do your duty!—Editor's translation]

In the subsequent interrogatory we learn the distance of this threat (fifteen meters or so), its state of rest or motion (motionless), its sex (presumably a boy), its occupation (sitting on the ground as if leaning on something). Hamm, perhaps thinking of the resurrected Jesus, murmurs "La pierre levée," then on reflection changes the image to constitute himself proprietor of the Promised Land: "Il regarde la maison sans doute, avec les yeux de Moïse mourant." It is doing, however, nothing of the kind; it is gazing at its navel. There is no use, Hamm decides, in running out to exterminate it: "If he exists he'll die there or he'll come here. And if he doesn't . . ." And a few seconds later he has conceded the game:

It's the end, Clov, we've come to the end. I don't need you any more.

He sacrifices his last mobile piece, discards his staff and whistle, summons for the last time a resourceless Knight and an unanswering Pawn, and covers his face once more with the handkerchief: somehow in check.

Not that all this is likely to be yielded up with clarity by any conceivable performance. It represents however a structure which, however we glimpse it, serves to refrigerate the incidental passions of a play about, it would seem, the end of humanity. It is not for nothing that the place within which the frigid events are transacted is more than once called "the shelter," outside of which is death; nor that the human race is at present reduced to two disabled parents, a macabre blind son, and an acathisiac servant. Around this shelter the universe crumbles away like an immense dry biscuit: no more rugs, no more tide, no more coffins. We hear of particular deaths:

> *Clov* (*harshly*). When old Mother Pegg asked you for oil for her lamp and you told her to get out to hell, you knew what was happening then, no? (*Pause.*) You know what she died of, Mother Pegg? Of darkness.
>
> *Hamm* (*feebly*). I hadn't any.
>
> *Clov* (*as before*). Yes, you had.

We observe particular brutalities: Hamm, of his parents: "Have you bottled her?" "Yes." "Are they both bottled?" "Yes." "Screw down the lids." What has shrunken the formerly ample world is perhaps Hamm's withdrawal of love; the great skull-like setting suggests a solipsist's universe. "I was never there," he says. "Absent, always. It all happened without me. I don't know what's happened." He has been in "the shelter"; he has also been closed within himself. It is barely possible that the desolation is not universal:

> *Hamm.* Did you ever think of one thing?
>
> *Clov.* Never.
>
> *Hamm.* That here we're down in a hole. (*Pause.*) But beyond the hills? Eh? Perhaps it's still green. Eh? (*Pause.*) Flora! Pomona! (*Ecstatically.*) Ceres! (*Pause.*) Perhaps you won't need to go very far.
>
> *Clov.* I can't go very far. (*Pause.*) I'll leave you.

As Hamm is both chessman and chess player, so it is conceivable that destruction is not screened off by the shelter but radiates from it for a certain distance. Zero, zero, words we hear so often in the dialogue, these are the Cartesian coordinates of the origin.

Bounded in a nutshell yet king of infinite space, Hamm articulates the racking ambiguity of the play by means of his dominance over its most persuasive metaphor, the play itself. If he is Prospero with staff and revels, if he is Richard III bloodsmeared and crying "My kingdom for a nightman!" if he is also perhaps Richard II, within whose hollow crown

> . . . Keeps Death his court, and there the Antic sits,
> Scoffing his state and grinning at his pomp,
> Allowing him a breath, a little scene
> To monarchize, be feared, and kill with looks—[3]

[3] I owe this suggestion to Mr. Walker's article.

these roles do not exhaust his repertoire. He is (his name tells us) the generic Actor, a creature all circumference and no center. As master of the revels, he himself attends to the last unveiling of the opening ritual:

> (*Pause. Hamm stirs. He yawns under the handkerchief. He removes the handkerchief from his face. Very red face, black glasses.*)
>
> *Hamm.* Me—(*he yawns*)—to play. (*He holds the handkerchief spread out before him.*) Old stancher! (. . . *He clears his throat, joins the tips of his fingers.*) Can there be misery—(*he yawns*)—loftier than mine?

The play ended, he ceremoniously unfolds the handkerchief once more (five separate stage directions governing his tempo) and covers his face as it was in the beginning. "Old Stancher! (*Pause.*) You . . . remain." What remains, in the final brief tableau specified by the author, is the immobile figure with a bloodied Veronica's veil in place of a face: the actor having superintended his own Passion and translated himself into an ultimate abstraction of masked agony.

Between these termini he animates everything, ordering the coming and going of Clov and the capping and uncapping of the cans. When Clov asks, "What is there to keep me here?" he answers sharply, "The dialogue." A particularly futile bit of business with the spyglass and the steps elicits from him an aesthetic judgment, "This is deadly." When it is time for the introduction of the stuffed dog, he notes, "We're getting on," and a few minutes later, "Do you not think this has gone on long enough?" These, like comparable details in *Godot,* are sardonic authorizations for a disquiet that is certainly stirring in the auditorium. No one understands better than Beckett, nor exploits more boldly, the kind of fatalistic attention an audience trained on films is accustomed to place at the dramatist's disposal. The cinema has taught us to suppose that a dramatic presentation moves inexorably as the reels unwind or the studio clock creeps, until it has consumed precisely its allotted time which nothing, no restlessness in the pit, no sirens, no mass exodus can hurry. "Something is taking its course," that suffices us. Hence the vast leisure in which the minimal business of *Godot* and *Endgame* is transacted; hence (transposing into dramatic terms the author's characteristic pedantry of means) the occasional lingering over points of technique, secure in the knowledge that the clock-bound patience of a twentieth-century audience will expect no inner urgency, nothing in fact but the actual time events consume, to determine the pace of the exhibition. Clov asks, "Why this farce, day after day?" and it is sufficient for Hamm to reply, "Routine. One never knows." It is the answer of an actor in an age of films and long runs. In *Endgame* (which here differs radically from *Godot*) no one is supposed to be improvising; the script has been well committed to memory and well rehearsed. By this means doom is caused to penetrate the most intimate crevices of the play. "I'm tired of going on," says Clov late in the play, "very tired," and then, "Let's stop playing!" (if there is one thing that modern acting is not it is playing). In the final moments theatrical technique, under Hamm's sponsorship, rises into savage prominence.

> *Hamm.* . . . And me? Did anyone ever have pity on me?
> *Clov* (*lowering the telescope, turning towards Hamm*). What? (*Pause.*) Is it me you're referring to?
> *Hamm* (*angrily*). An aside, ape! Did you never hear an aside before? (*Pause.*) I'm warming up for my last soliloquy.

Ten seconds later he glosses "More complications!" as a technical term: "Not an underplot, I trust." It is Clov who has the last word in this vein:

> *Hamm.* Clov! (*Clov halts, without turning.*) Nothing. (*Clov moves on.*) Clov! (*Clov halts, without turning.*)
> *Clov.* This is what we call making an exit.

By this reiterated stress on the actors as professional men, and so on the play as an occasion within which they operate, Beckett transforms Hamm's last soliloquy into a performance, his desolation into something prepared by the dramatic machine, his abandoning of gaff, dog, and whistle into a necessary discarding of props, and the terminal business with the handkerchief into, quite literally, a curtain speech. *Endgame* ends with an unexpected lightness, a death rather mimed than experienced; if it is "Hamm as stated, and Clov as stated, together as stated," the mode of statement has more salience than a paraphrase of the play's situation would lead one to expect.

The professionalism also saves the play from an essentially sentimental committment to simpliste "destiny." Much of its gloomy power it derives from contact with such notions as T. H. Huxley's view of man as an irrelevance whom day by day an indifferent universe engages in chess. We do not belong here, runs a strain of Western thought which became especially articulate in France after the War; we belong nowhere; we are all surds, ab-surd. There is nothing on which to ground our right to exist, and we need not be especially surprised one day to find ourselves nearly extinct. (On such a despair Cartesian logic converges, as surely as the arithmetic of Pythagoras wedged itself fast in the irrationality of $\sqrt{2}$.) Whatever we do, then, since it can obtain no grip on our radically pointless situation, is *behavior* pure and simple; it is play acting, and may yield us the satisfaction, if satisfaction there be, of playing well, of uttering our *cris du coeur* with style and some sense of timing. We do not trouble deaf heaven, for there is only the sky ("Rien," reports Clov, gazing through his telescope; and again, "Zéro.") We stir and thrill, at best, ourselves. From such a climate, miscalled existentialist, Beckett wrings every available *frisson* without quite delivering the play into its keeping; for its credibility is not a principle the play postulates but an idea the play contains, an idea of which it works out the moral and spiritual consequences. The despair in which he traffics is a conviction, not a philosophy. He will even set it spinning like a catharine wheel about a wild point of logic, as when he has Hamm require that God be prayed to in silence ("Where are your manners?") and then berate him ("The bastard!") for not existing.[4]

The play contains whatever ideas we discern inside it; no idea contains the play. The play contains, moreover, two narrative intervals, performances within the performance. The first, Nagg's story about the trousers, is explicitly a recitation; Nell has heard it often, and so, probably, has the audience; it is a vaudeville standby. Nagg's performance, like a production of *King Lear,* whose story we know, must therefore be judged solely as a performance. Its quality, alas, discourages even him ("I tell this story worse and worse."), and Nell too is not amused, being occupied with thoughts of her own, about the sand at the bottom of Lake Como. The other is Hamm's huffe-snuffe narrative, also a recitation, since we are to gather that he has been composing it beforehand, in his head. This time we do not know the substance of the tale, but contemplate in diminishing perspective an actor who has memorized a script which enjoins him to imitate a man who has devised and memorized a script:

> The man came crawling towards me, on his belly. Pale, wonderfully pale and thin, he seemed on the point of—(*Pause. Normal tone.*) No, I've done that bit.

Later on he incorporates a few critical reflections: "Nicely put, that," or "There's English for you." This technician's narcissism somewhat disinfects the dreadful tale. All Hamm's satisfactions come from dramatic self-contemplation, and as he towers before us, devoid of mercy, it is to some ludicrous stage villain that he assimilates himself, there on the stage, striking a stage-Barabbas pose ("Sometimes I go about and poison wells."). It is to this that life as play-acting comes.

[4] The Lord Chamberlain, a less subtle (or less orthodox) theologian, required that for performances on the English stage "bastard" should be altered to "swine."

> In the end he asked me would I consent to take in the child as well—if he were still alive. (*Pause.*) It was the moment I was waiting for. (*Pause.*) Would I consent to take in the child. . . . (*Pause.*) I can see him still, down on his knees, his hands flat on the ground, glaring at me with his mad eyes, in defiance of my wishes.

"It was the moment I was waiting for": the satisfaction this exudes is considerably less sadistic than dramatic, and the anticlimax into which the long performance immediately topples would try a creator's soul, not a maniac's:

> I'll soon have finished with this story. (*Pause.*) Unless I bring in other characters. (*Pause.*) But where would I find them? (*Pause.*) Where would I look for them? (*Pause. He whistles. Enter Clov.*) Let us pray to God.

So the hooks go in. There is no denying what Beckett called in a letter to Alan Schneider "the power of the text to claw." It strikes, however, its unique precarious balance between rage and art, immobilizing all characters but one, rotating before us for ninety unbroken minutes the surfaces of Nothing, always designedly faltering on the brink of utter insignificance into which nevertheless we cannot but project so many awful significances: theater reduced to its elements in order that theatricalism may explore without mediation its own boundaries: a bleak unforgettable tour de force and probably its author's single most remarkable work.

Hamm, Clov, and Dramatic Method in *Endgame*

by Antony Easthope

One way in which a play holds the attention of an audience for the duration of its performance is by presenting an action which may be formulated as a question: Who killed Laius? How will Hamlet revenge his father? *Endgame* has a plot at least to the extent that it holds its audience with an uncertainty, one which is continuously reiterated from the stage: Will Clov leave Hamm? At the end, when the final tableau shows Clov standing there, with umbrella, raincoat, and bag, unable to stay and unable to go, the question remains unresolved. Nevertheless, any discussion of *Endgame,* including one which proposes to consider the play's dramatic method, should begin with this question, or rather with the relationship between Hamm and Clov from which it arises. And since Clov is for the most part a passive victim, a pawn dominated by Hamm's active mastery, it is with Hamm that we should start.

In order to get even as far as the play will let us towards understanding why Hamm keeps Clov (assuming that he could in fact let him go), we must try to see what Hamm is like. He is like a king, with Clov as his servant, for he refers to "my house,"[1] "my service," and even, echoing Shakespeare's Richard III, to "my kingdom." On one occasion he uses the royal plural to Clov, "You can't leave us." In a former time he had real power, or so he claims, when Clov, as he reminds him, "inspected my paupers." Now his realm has shrunk almost to nothing and he is left with Clov, Nagg, and Nell as his courtiers. His relationship with Clov is like that between Pozzo and Lucky in *Godot,* and its quality is well conveyed by Lionel Abel's suggestion

---

"Hamm, Clov, and Dramatic Method in Endgame*" by Antony Easthope. From* Modern Drama, X *(Spring, 1968), 424–33.*

[1] Samuel Beckett, *Endgame, A Play in One Act followed by Act without Words, A Mime for One Player,* trans. by the author (New York, 1958).

that it is an analogue of the relationship between the young Beckett and the old, blind, Joyce. Hamm treats Nagg and Nell as further objects for gratuitous affliction—"Bottle him!" Hamm seems to be a tyrant, who lives to enjoy the exercise of his power over others. But it is at this point that the difficulties begin, for to say that Hamm enjoys exercising power is to attribute a familiar form of psychological motivation to him—and it is hard to be sure he has the capacity for this. Together with its many other connotations, Hamm is the name for an actor, for one who creates an identity which has only an imaginary existence. And the tone of what Hamm says is frequently consistent with that of an assumed identity, one deliberately acted out. So he deals with the requests of his servants:

Clov. He wants a sugar-plum.
Hamm. He'll get a sugar-plum.

Hamm's reply is such a fulsome expression of largesse and arrogant condescension that it seems merely a verbal gesture. Nagg does not get his sugar-plum, but what we might take to be Hamm's intentional malice cannot properly be distinguished from a pretence of high-handed magnificence which is part of the role he plays. Hamm orders Clov to screw down the lids of the ashbins on Nagg and Nell, and then comments on himself, "My anger subsides, I'd like to pee." It is this continuous self-consciousness in Hamm's words and tone of voice which inhibits us from ascribing his cruelty to an impulse beyond the need for rhetorical coherence in the role he plays.

Hamm appears to suffer, but with this there is the same doubt as with his cruelty. While introducing himself, Hamm proclaims his agony:

> Can there be misery—(*he yawns*)—loftier than mine? No doubt. Formerly. But now?

His expression of "loftier misery" is laden with echoes of Oedipus the King and of Christ as presented in Herbert's poem, *The Sacrifice,* with the famous refrain, "Was ever grief like to mine?" The salt of genuine affliction dissolves among these overtones into a self-conscious rhetoric, a heavy irony directed at the very possibility of real suffering. Hamm takes the magnitude of his "misery" as guarantee for the importance of his role. On several occasions in the play introspection leads him to talk as though he were suffering, but each time his words become a performance. When Hamm speaks of a heart dripping in his head, he is exposed immediately to the ridicule of Nagg and Nell, who react to his unhappiness as a fiction, ". . . it's like the funny story we have heard too often." Later Hamm tells Clov that he too will go blind one day and find himself alone in "infinite emptiness"—but this again may be seen as an act, a set speech which the stage directions mark as to be performed *"With prophetic relish."* Beckett has written of *Endgame* that it is "more inhuman than 'Godot' "[2] and Hamm's cruelty earns the play this adjective. But it may be understand in a double sense. In so far as Hamm is felt as a real character, then he is inhuman in the sense we use the word of a man whose actions are so extreme that they seem to place him beyond the pale of humanity. His boundless cynicism may be seen as a desperate attempt to anticipate the cruelty of a universe which is indifferent to his wishes, and his expressions of suffering may be symptoms of genuine agony. Thus, in his hatred of "life," Hamm becomes like King Lear, who, when stripped of all he values, can only cry, "Then kill, kill, kill, kill, kill, kill." To describe Hamm's putative character in such melodramatic language is an appropriate response to the play, for all this may be no more than an aspect of his deliberate playacting. Hamm may in fact be inhuman only in the strict sense of being not human, if the fiction of his role is so perfectly sustained that it excludes any capacity for genuine motive and what we take to be real humanity. Such perhaps is the implication of Hamm's admission to Clov, "I was never there," though this depends upon the stress an actor gives to the personal pronoun. So a full account of Hamm must comprehend both the surface fiction of his role and the psychological depths suggested beneath it. And the main event in *Endgame,* Hamm's story, manifests this ambiguity or doubleness with a clarity which must be considered in detail.

Hamm's story may be seen as a fictional extension of his role, demonstrating clearly how conscious he is of the part he plays. He fancies himself as a great lord, a Pharaoh or a Czar. A father comes to him, begging some corn for a starving child. With enormous complacency the master waits for the end of the plea, for the most dramatic moment, before giving his crushing reply:

> Use your head, can't you, use your head, you're on earth, there's no cure for that!

This fantasy account of the exercise of power seems no more than a perfect opportunity for Hamm to practise his histrionic talents. Yet there are many suggestions in the telling of the story which imply that Hamm is seriously involved and that his fiction reflects real anxiety and suffering. For, latent beneath the surface of his chronicle, a tenuous connection of metaphors and phrases repeated in different con-

[2] See, "Beckett's Letters on *Endgame*: Extracts from his Correspondence with Director Alan Schneider," *The Village Voice Reader,* ed. Daniel Wolf and Edwin Fancher (New York, 1962), pp. 182–186.

texts renders Hamm's relationship with Clov as the hidden subject of his story.

Throughout the play Clov is likened to a dog. He refers to his birth as being "whelped;" he comes to Hamm when he whistles, and the master wears a whistle round his neck for this purpose. Great play is made with a stage-prop, a stuffed dog, and once Clov hands this to Hamm with the revealing plural, "Your dogs are here." Clov stands continually, he cannot sit, and Hamm is concerned that the stuffed animal should be able to stand. Like Clov, the dog cannot leave, "He's not a real dog, he can't go." But, as we discover, the function of the toy dog for Hamm is to enlarge his role, bolstering his grandeur by standing there imploring him, "as if he were begging . . . for a bone." Through the figures of dog and beggar, Hamm's relationship to Clov becomes transposed into his story. So also with the reference to a child. Clov is Hamm's child, or at least, Hamm "was a father" to him. Hamm tells Clov he will give him just enough to keep him from dying, so that, like the starving boy in the story, Clov will be "hungry all the time." At the end, when Clov says he sees a small boy approaching, Hamm tells him he will need him no longer, implying that the small boy will take Clov's place. Thus Hamm's violent pronouncement to the beggar and his child is felt as though spoken to Clov. Twice elsewhere in the play Hamm says "Use your head," on both occasions while addressing Clov.

It may be that Hamm keeps coming back to his story simply in the interest of art. For the *raconteur* practice makes perfect, and Hamm appears to think his only concern with the anecdote is to polish its phrasing—"Technique, you know." But it is hard not to respond to the way he returns again and again to his story as symptomatic of a genuine obsession with it. If this is so, it is consistent with the character suggested behind Hamm's role. The telling of the story looks like a guilty attempt by Hamm to convince himself that nihilism justifies hardness of heart, ". . . you're on earth, there's no cure for that!" Guilt would result if Hamm feared that his cynicism were merely a rationalization for a cruel impulse prior to it, and Clov awakens exactly this fear later in the play, the effect being to drive Hamm almost into silence:

> *Clov* (*harshly*). When old Mother Pegg asked you for oil for her lamp and you told her to get out to hell, you knew what was happening then, no? (*Pause.*) You know what she died of, Mother Pegg? Of darkness.
>
> *Hamm* (*feebly*). I hadn't any.
>
> *Clov* (*as before*). Yes, you had.

That Hamm's story disturbs him at a level which he cannot—or will not—recognize is implied by what follows it in the rest of the play. Immediately after Hamm's story the famous prayer to God takes place. Perhaps this is another facet of Hamm's role, another fiction, since it is prefaced by his remark that he may need "other characters." Or again, it may be a symptom of remorse and an authentic quest for grace, particularly if Hamm has remembered the Biblical parable echoed in his story, that of Dives and Lazarus, and thought of the appalling punishment meted out to the cruel master at the end of that. Earlier Hamm had made a jocular reference to Clov's kissing him goodbye before leaving; after the story the motif recurs, but this time Hamm's phrasing sounds personally insistent:

Hamm. Kiss me. (*Pause.*) Will you not kiss me?

Is this another patronising demand for homage, dictated by the master's role? Or are we to detect in it a lurking desire for forgiveness? All through the play Hamm has nagged Clov for his pain-killer; on the single occasion he repeats his request after the story, he is answered in the affirmative, and then told by Clov, "There's no more pain-killer." Hamm's reaction to this seems to be the hysteria of uncontrollable agony:

Hamm (*soft*). What'll I do? (*Pause. In a scream.*) What'll I do?

Yet the violence of this disappears in his next words to Clov, "What are you doing?" Anaphora smooths over the expressive intensity of Hamm's cry, making it seem less a cry of pain and more like a mere ruffle in the verbal surface. At the end of the play Clov's reported sighting of a small boy is followed by Hamm's final soliloquy, which contains a last reference to his story, "If he could have his child with him."

What this argument has tried to show is that Hamm has a double nature, existing both as consciously played role and as real character. His role as king and master seems to be unbroken and self-contained. Any subject to which he directs his attention, even his own suffering, becomes falsified through absorption into conscious rhetoric and turned into the performance of an actor. Yet there is something more about Hamm, which escapes his attention, a network of possibilities, a string of metaphorical connections and repeated phrases, leading beyond the role he knows he is playing. This implies obliquely a psychological reality in him, one which would perhaps evaporate into fiction if Hamm were able to give it explicit articulation. And this ambivalent relationship between surface and depth in the way that

Hamm is dramatised is worked out as a structural principle in the whole of *Endgame*. The depths of the play, its metaphorical and suggestive qualities, have occupied the attention of most critics of the play. Hugh Kenner in his book on Beckett and also Robert Benedetti in a recent article for the *Chicago Review* have shown how the play is aware of itself as a text performed in a theater. It is sufficient to list the technical theatrical terms used in it in order to remark the rigor with which this effect is created: "farce," "audition," "aside," "soliloquy," "dialogue," "underplot," "exit." The result of these references is that many lines come to sound as comments on the play made from the stage, "This is slow work," and so on. But if *Endgame* contains a consciousness of itself as a theatrical performance generated according to the conventions of that form, this is only part of the whole. For the verbal surface of the play is pervaded by a deliberate sense of artifice, which never allows an audience to forget they are watching a game played according to certain rules. As Hamm says, "Since that's the way we're playing it . . . let's play it that way." And a principal effect of the drama derives from the deft manner in which a consciously sustained surface, itself a meaningless exercise in various techniques, is held in tension with the expressive significance of what is suggested beneath it.

One of the most unusual rhetorical techniques which occurs in *Endgame* is this:

Nagg. I had it yesterday.
Nell (*elegiac*). Ah yesterday! (*They turn painfully towards each other.*)

A little later the same turn is again given to the word "yesterday" in an exchange between Nagg and Nell. A word from the first speaker's sentence is repeated with an exclamation mark in reply. The effect in both these cases is, as the stage directions make clear, to parody sentimental evocation. On another occasion the tone is marked to imply scepticism:

Clov (*dismayed*). Looks like a small boy!
Hamm (*sarcastic*). A small . . . boy!

But when it is not discriminated by the directions the tone of the exclamation must combine contempt, scepticism and sadness. The function of the device seems to be to sterilise an emotional gesture by questioning assumptions it contains. Thus it is perfectly placed at a point when the dialogue discusses just such a movement as the turn of phrase enacts:

Hamm. We're not beginning to . . . to . . . mean something?
Clov. Mean something! You and I, mean something! (*Brief laugh.*) That's a good one!

By the end of the play the device has become a cliché, and thus when it is used twice on the mention of a heart as Hamm and Clov exchange goodbyes, the exclamation has been robbed of most of the force it had as an assertive protest:

Hamm. A few words . . . to ponder . . . in my heart.
Clov. Your heart!

Of course what Hamm says may be a sincere plea for kindness from Clov, just as his reply may be taken to express bitter contempt for the way he has been exploited by the master. But it would be a misreading of the play to respond to the emotional significance of the exchanges without recognising that this is entirely subordinated to what is now a stock response, a merely verbal gesture. The rhythm of this rhetorical device is insidious and easily acquired by a good ear; it contributes a great deal to the unique resonance of the play.

The verbal surface of *Endgame* is aware of itself as being organized in accordance with the conventions governing conversation and stage dialogue, particularly a kind of two person dialogue not unlike that of the old music-hall tradition of the comic and the straight-man. The conversational form admits several kinds of monologue, and these are performed as such. Two anecdotes are available to eke out the entertainment, Hamm's story and Nagg's joke about the Englishman and the tailor. This he is directed to pronounce in a "(*Raconteur's voice.*)" Hamm, as the best talker on the stage, has the largest repertoire of monologues. Besides anecdote he is also capable of the philosophic speculation, "Imagine if a rational being came back to earth . . . ," and, with a sense of *tour de force,* the prophetic admonition, "One day you'll say to yourself . . . ," which he declaims for Clov. In each case the significant undertones are ignored by the surface, so that even Hamm's frightening account of the madman who saw the beauty of the world as ashes is presented as a formal exercise, it being of course that standby of conversation, the reminiscence:

Clov. A madman? When was that?
Hamm. Oh way back, way back, you weren't in the land of the living.

The language of Clov's last speech at the end of the play describes with delicate and appalling precision the feelings of a man released after a lifetime of imprisonment:

> I open the door of the cell and go. I am so bowed I only see my feet, if I open my eyes, and between my legs a little trail of black dust. I say to myself that the world is extinguished, though I never saw it lit. (*Pause.*) It's easy going. (*Pause.*) When I fall I'll weep for happiness.

Yet the stage directions insist that the evocative power of this language is to be deliberately suppressed: "CLOV (*fixed gaze, tonelessly, towards auditorium*)." The speech is, as Clov reminds us, the correct theatrical gesture for making an exit. For this, as for the other monologues, including Hamm's self-styled "last soliloquy," the play will accept no responsibility beyond that for applying certain theatrical and conversational conventions.

The dialogue of *Endgame* is a brilliantly contrived exercise in the art of repartee. Unfortunately, discussion of a single passage, one of the best, will have to stand for analysis of a quality of conscious formal elegance which pervades the whole:

> *Hamm.* Nature has forgotten us.
> *Clov.* There's no more nature.
> *Hamm.* No more nature! You exaggerate.
> *Clov.* In the vicinity.
> *Hamm.* But we breathe, we change! We lose our hair, our teeth! Our bloom! Our ideals!
> *Clov.* Then she hasn't forgotten us.
> *Hamm.* But you say there is none.
> *Clov* (*sadly*). No one that ever lived ever thought so crooked as we.
> *Hamm.* We do what we can.
> *Clov.* We shouldn't.

The issue behind this exchange is clear enough—whether Nature and Nature's God have temporarily withdrawn themselves from man or have actually ceased to exist. But serious concern with this question is submerged in this sharp, witty, paradoxical dialogue, often dependent on the interplay of verbal connection and logical non-sequitur, which is of a kind that has fascinated the Irish from Swift to Shaw. Hamm's straight-man assertion provokes Clov's stock response, "There's no more Nature." His denial is categorical in form, an either/or, but Hamm impossibly calls it an exaggeration, at the same time employing a rhetorical exclamation made familiar by the rest of the play. Hamm's response, instead of collapsing the conversation, elicits an equally impossible concession from Clov, "In the vicinity," as though Nature, if it existed, could exist locally but not universally. This Hamm ignores, launching into the vigorous if paradoxical proof that universal decay is evidence for Nature's continued existence. Instead of replying to this in terms consistent with his previous denial, Clov counters wittily by accepting the existence of human decay as evidence of Nature's benevolence, "Then she hasn't forgotten us." Hamm takes this to be Clov's admission that he was wrong, a move which Clov tries to thwart with a sententious aphorism, "No one that ever lived thought so crooked as we." Hamm pounces on this by implying that crooked thinking is all to the good. But his words are ambiguous, for "can" here means both "the best we can" and "what we have to do." Thus the Parthian shaft comes from Clov, who outwits Hamm by repeating his disapproval of crooked thinking in a way which supposes that people do by choice what Hamm has unintentionally said they do by necessity. After a pause, this vigorous little canter earns Clov his master's praise, "You're a bit of all right, aren't you?" This adapts the vulgar British phrase as admiration for Clov's high technical proficiency in playing games with a concept whose varying definitions have worried thinkers of our civilization for over two thousand years. It is because of a similar delight in technical expertise that Hamm on a later occasion cannot resist self-congratulation:

Clov. Do you believe in the life to come?
Hamm. Mine was always that. (*Exit Clov.*) Got him that time!

Once again, a serious subject, the fate of man's external soul, is used mainly as an occasion for repartee, and this juxtaposition of a formal surface with serious, often terrifying depths accounts for much of what Beckett in his correspondence with Alan Schneider referred to as "the power of the text to claw."

A word frequently applied to Beckett's work is "poetic." What the adjective really points to in Beckett's plays (a context in which it is pejorative if it replaces the honorific qualification "dramatic") is the extra-ordinary ability of the language and stage-craft to imply, suggest, connote, evoke, and set off expressive nuances. In this respect *Endgame* fulfills expectations which derive to us from our experience of the Symbolist tradition in poetry and drama, for it was Mallarmé's principle that "to name is to destroy; to suggest is to create." It is this, and the traditional assumption that drama imitates a reality beyond itself, which Beckett has chosen to exploit. And he exploits it by providing the play with a level of action, which ignores its own significant implications. The surface of *Endgame* insists upon itself as a meaningless technical exercise of the medium in its own right and refuses to acknowledge anything beyond its own expertise. Beckett stresses this in his own comment on the play, again in a letter to Alan Schneider:

> My work is a matter of fundamental sounds (no joke intended) made as fully as possible, and I accept responsibility for nothing else. If people want to have headaches among the overtones, let them. And provide their own aspirin. Hamm as stated, and Clov as stated, together as stated, nec tecum nec sine te, in such a place, and in such a world, that's all I can manage, more than I could.

The life of *Endgame* is in the tension it creates by the harsh juxtaposition of the depths and the surface, the "overtones" and what is stated, a doubleness which is apparent in the frequent pauses in the play. On the one hand these are hushed silences in which the resonances of the text may vibrate and amplify in the mind of the audience—"God," "light," "Nature," "ended." At the same time these pauses are merely technical requirements, rests between moves in the last game which is *Endgame,* no more, no less. Thus the dramatic structure of the play enacts a dialectic which Beckett has stated elsewhere—in *Watt,* his second novel—as, "this pursuit of meaning, in this indifference to meaning." In so far as we recognise this as an insight into the conditions of human existence we will be able to respond to the full effect of *Endgame.*

An Approach to *Endgame*[1]

by Ross Chambers

Der Stoff ist nicht der Zweck der Kunst, aber die Ausführung ist es.

Novalis

"It is not subject-matter that is the goal of art," one reads in *Heinrich von Ofterdingen,* "but performance," which perhaps means that ideally subject and execution ought to be one, as they are in music. Or as they are in *Endgame,* a play whose meaning lies in its performance, since it organises movement, gesture and speech in time and space so as to form a structure. Such a structure, of course, *means* what it *is,* but it also, as Sartre suggests, implies a metaphysic and forms an image of our life of movement, gesture and speech. There is, as it were, a concealed metaphor, of which we are given one pole only (the vehicle), together with some hints, so fragmentary and inexplicit that their primary function is perhaps to suggest that an allusion is being made rather than to specify that allusion, but which nonetheless orientate the spectator towards an interpretation. It is for us—if we wish, and if we can—to guess at the other pole of the metaphor (the tenor) and define it if we can. The guesses may well be highly subjective; they will be correct to the extent that they respect the structure Beckett has given us and justify it. Other interpretations, however divergent they may appear, will be complementary if they do likewise.

The play is first and foremost what we see: the space set out before

---

"An Approach to Endgame" *by Ross Chambers [Original title: "Vers une interpretation de* Fin de Partie"]. Studi Francesi, *no. 31 (gennaio-aprile, 1967), 90–96.* *Translated and revised by the author. Reprinted in revised translation by permission of the author and* Studi Francesi.

[1] In rewriting my original French ("Vers une interprétation de *Fin de Partie*", *Studi Francesi,* 31, gennaio-aprile 1967), I have taken the opportunity of making some minor changes with a view to clarifying the argument and minimising repetition of points I have made elsewhere.

us. In *Endgame,* there are two spaces, one which is seen and one which is described, and seen—by the audience, as by Hamm—only through the eyes of another: an inner space, then, whose reality is a matter of immediate observation, and a world without, which we have to take on trust. Between the two is a wall, with two windows and a door. I am not the first to be reminded of Malone lying in a room which is perhaps his own head, and to identify the windows with eyes of some sort.[2] But this being so, then the door—which communicates not with the external world but with the kitchen, Clov's domain—becomes some kind of mouth, the means of communication with other people as the eyes are our windows on the world. The difference is that other people, unlike the earth and sea, are not content to remain outside: Clov comes and goes freely in Hamm's domain, and two others, Nagg and Nell, have actually set up residence there permanently, perhaps for ever. What are we to make of this inner world which is, on the one hand, so clearly partitioned off and on the other open to invasion from without?

One might, of course, see in it an image of the dualistic conception of subject and object of consciousness, of self and nonself, which we have inherited from Descartes. "Old wall!" says Hamm, in the course of his voyage "round the world," "beyond is the . . . other hell" (p. 26).[3] But the wall is itself a source of perplexity and disturbance to Hamm, for it is curiously hollow. He feels it, applies his ear to it: "Do you hear? Hollow bricks! (*He strikes again.*) All that's hollow!" (p. 26). The line of demarcation between the inner and the outer hell is problematical, and more fragile than it at first appears; in a sense it does not really exist, or it exists and does not exist at one and the same time; it affirms but also casts doubt on the separation of the inner and the outer worlds. For the Cartesian concept is a satisfying one so long as one can assign the self a well-defined situation in space, as Descartes did by placing it somewhat arbitrarily in the pineal gland. Three centuries later it has become difficult to accept this solution, and our conviction concerning the existence of a separate and separable self has been somewhat shaken by the problem of locating it in physical space. How can one continue to believe in one's "selfhood" if one does not know *where* one is? And yet, how shake off the conviction that one

[2] Cf. Hugh Kenner, *Samuel Beckett, A Critical Study* (London, Calder, 1962), p. 155: "(. . .) we fancy the stage, with its high peepholes, to be the inside of an immense skull." [See this voluume, p. 53.]

[3] Reference throughout is to Samuel Beckett, *Endgame* (New York, Grove Press, 1958). Allusions to the French text refer to *Fin de Partie* (Paris, Editions de Minuit, 1957).

is? This doubt, this problem of circumscription is raised by the ambiguous reality of the wall in Hamm's room.

Can one conceive of a self not circumscribed by a wall, existing, but existing independently of space? If one clings to the idea of separate selfhood, distinguishable from the world around it, and if one is not prepared to conceive of it in dynamic terms (as a function rather than a place), then one must imagine it existing outside of the world of physical extension, in a "place" that is somehow non-spatial; and one may draw an analogy from the idea of the center of a circle, which we know to exist, but which exists ideally, and is in no way to be confused with its crude geometrical representation in the form of a dot. Just such a "dot" is Hamm, who as a character offers us the outer shell of an inner being we cannot see, a kind of mental space situated *inside* the room or head he lives in, circumscribed by his physical frame, it is true, but free, as the room is not, of invasion from without. Blind Hamm is separate from the world around him, a world at whose exact center he imagines himself to be,[4] but he is not separated by anything so crude as a wall:

> One day you'll be blind, like me [he says to Clov]. You'll be sitting there, a speck in the void, in the dark, forever, like me. (. . .) One day (. . .) you'll look at the wall a while, then you'll say, I'll close my eyes (. . .). And when you open them again there'll be no wall any more. (*Pause.*) Infinite emptiness will be all around you, all the resurrected dead of all ages wouldn't fill it, and there you'll be like a little bit of grit in the middle of the steppe. (p. 36)

In becoming blind, Hamm, it is clear, has achieved a measure of freedom from spatial reality (and the image of the resurrected dead is not coincidental); he thinks of himself as a tiny plenum in the surrounding void (*petit plein perdu dans le vide,* as the French text says), but one which is not defined by a wall. It is worth noticing that in such an interpretation his blindness (and, one may add, his paralysis) are not to be thought of as mere signs of physical decadence but as stages in progress towards discovery of self. If he could walk, Hamm would still be at the stage of Clov's absurd comings and goings, and would not have reached his position at the center of the world; if he could see, he would still be in contact with the outer world, and the boundary of his inner domain would be set far from its mid-point, at the hol-

[4] HAMM: Am I right in the center? CLOV: I'll measure it. HAMM: More or less! More or less! CLOV (*moving chair slightly*): There! HAMM: I'm more or less in the center? CLOV: I'd say so. HAMM: You'd say so! Put me right in the center! (. . . etc.) (pp. 26–7).

low brick wall of his skull. But it is clear also that Hamm has not succeeded in completely leaving behind him the world of space; he sees himself as a wall-less plenum, but the spectators see only the wall of his body and are dependent on his words for information about the self within. And the very power of speech, which gives evidence of selfhood, itself constantly betrays that same selfhood by serving as a means of communication with the world without. Hamm is sightless and motionless, but not yet silent; he has shattered the windows of his inner world, but the door remains open and the world of others still exists for him. He is not a center but a dot, imprisoned in the shell of his body which *represents* for us what Hamm has not yet succeeded in *being*.

He is, however, closer to the goal than Clov, and that is why it is important to consider the time-world of the play as well as its structure in space. When we observe the three generations of people on stage, it is evident that self-discovery involves a long process of abstraction from the world—casting off the external trappings of existence, abandoning movement for motionlessness, narrowing the space in which one lives—a process which fills a lifetime so lengthy it seems to go on for ever, and perhaps does. For Clov, Hamm's servant and/or son, is still very young, in spite of his great age and physical decrepitude; he is still very far from the goal. He is relatively active, being not yet motionless; he looks out on the external world, being not yet blind; and he still lives in a world of objects—telescopes, alarm-clocks, stools and the like. He conceives the end he is striving for as a departure and a voyage, and in the last moments of the play is seen equipped with panama hat, tweed coat, raincoat, umbrella and bag—all of which he will have to be rid of before he reaches even the stage represented by Hamm. For Hamm, however blind, however restricted to his chair, is far from the ideal by comparison with his own parents: he remains susceptible to the charms of movement and has Clov push him about in his wheel-chair; he is still interested in the external universe as Clov reports it to him; and he too is still attached to objects such as his whistle, his toy-dog and his handkerchief, not to mention his urgent need for the presence of, and for speech with, his fellows, Clov, Nagg and Nell. His "accursed progenitors" in their turn have lost all interest in the outer world described by Clov, their universe is restricted to the inner world of Hamm's room, which in addition they perceive but dimly thanks to their failing sight and hearing. They live almost entirely within themselves—but they have not lost all interest in pap, biscuits and sugar-plums, they worry vaguely about the sand or sawdust that lines their dwellings, and above all they need to share with each other memories and kisses, the residue of their life. Enclosed in their dustbins, they are closer than anyone to the life at the ideal center, to the dream of absolute independence; but Beckett gives them, for example, the following snatch of dialogue:

Nagg. (. . .) Do you want to go in?
Nell. Yes.
Nagg. Then go in. (*Nell does not move.*) Why don't you go in?
Nell. I don't know. (p. 16)

Why is it so difficult to "go in"? That is the problem with which the whole play is concerned.

We have, then, three generations of old people whose lives are "over" but who are unable to reach their "end." They can neither arrive nor depart because they cannot "go in"; they can only wait. Is it death they are awaiting? Everything in the play suggests that death is a release that is forbidden them. They are "within," not so far within as they would wish, but nevertheless away from the outside world and protected by the hollow wall of Hamm's house. But death is a phenomenon of life "outside," of the deserted, moribund wasteland described periodically by Clov and at one point characterised by him as "corpsed" (p. 30). Out there Mother Pegg may well die "of darkness," her light "extinguished" (pp. 42 and 75); and when, towards the end, a child appears on the horizon, Hamm knows that "if he exists he'll die there or he'll come here" (p. 78), for, as he has already twice said, "outside of here it's death" (pp. 9 and 70). That is the alternative: to die in outside existence, or to come here, where there is hope of eventual "life," but where this hope is submerged in an agony of endlessness. For in this "other hell'" death is as impossible as any other ending, any other *achèvement* (the overtones of the pun are clearer in French):

Hamm. Why don't you finish us? (*Pause.*) I'll tell you the combination of the larder if you promise to finish me.
Clov. I couldn't finish you.
Hamm. Then you won't finish me. (p. 37)

Unable to die, like the rat half finished off in the kitchen, Hamm and his companions have to find another way out of this life, another salvation, and one which is perhaps very near:

Hamm. (. . .) And the rat?
Clov. He's got away.

Hamm. He can't go far. (*Pause. Anxious.*) Eh?
Clov. He doesn't need to go far. (pp. 70–71)

For Hamm has some intimation of a paradise beyond the hills:

Hamm. (. . .) Flora! Pomona! (*Ecstatically.*) Ceres! (*Pause.*) Perhaps you won't need to go very far.
Clov. I can't go very far. (p. 39)

That is the torment they are all condemned to: to be tantalisingly close to paradise, to a way out, to an end, but to be unable to reach it.

I have studied in another essay[5] the kind of time-world in which this desperate situation occurs, a world in which it is possible to edge nearer and nearer to the goal without ever attaining it. The reason for this impossibility lies in the definition of the goal. If, in space, the attempt to reach the self is like trying to become the center of a circle (a place outside of space), the attempt in time is equivalent to seeking a time outside of temporality, that is, eternity—for it is only outside of time (and space) that the self may exist free from contingency. But the attempt to reach eternity, like the attempt to reach the center, is an infinite process, the image of which in the play is a half-remembered paradox put forward by a pre-Socratic philosopher. Clov refers to it implicitly in the first speech of the play, in which we learn first that all is over, and then of his increasing suspicion that it is not, that it cannot be, that the desired "heap" is an impossible one:

Clov (*fixed gaze, tonelessly*). Finished, it's finished, nearly finished, it must be nearly finished. (*Pause.*) Grain upon grain, one by one, and one day, suddenly, there's a heap, a little heap, the impossible heap. (p. 1)

Like so many others in the play, these words are echoed later, by Hamm:

Moment upon moment, pattering down, like the millet grains of . . . (*he hesitates*) . . . that old Greek, and all life long you wait for that to mount up to a life. (*Pause. He opens his mouth to continue, renounces.*) Ah let's get it over! (p. 70)

The imprecision of the reference is characteristic of Beckett, but the allusion to the sorites of the infinitely increasing heap is clear enough for us to understand that the characters are aware of being engaged in a temporal process comparable to the infinite divisions or doublings dear to Zeno.[6]

[5] "Beckett's Brinkmanship," *AUMLA,* XIX (May 1963). Reprinted in *Samuel Beckett,* edited by Martin Esslin (Englewood Cliffs, N.J., Prentice-Hall, 1965).

[6] In "Beckett's Brinkmanship," I took Hamm's "old Greek" to be in fact Zeno. Mr. Beckett assures me that I am wrong, although, like Hamm, he cannot recall

The actual time-world into which the infinite process of approaching eternity leads is one of great ambiguity. Time appears to have slowed to a stop, so that when Hamm asks the hour, Clov is able to reply: "The same as usual" (p. 4); and a language that uses terms like "yesterday" seems almost meaningless (pp. 43–44). But in fact time has not stopped, something is "taking its course," albeit desperately slowly. The moments pass, pattering down one by one like the millet grains, each more slowly than the one before, but they pass; and at the end of the play all the characters have moved closer to the goal—Clov is ready to depart; Hamm has thrown away his gaff, his whistle, his dog; Nagg and Nell are much feebler than before. Time thus partakes both of eternity and of temporality, and its ambiguity corresponds to the ambiguous situation in space of Hamm's room, neither fully internal nor fully external (thanks to the "hollow" wall), lying somewhere between earth and sea, and filled with a grey crepuscular light which suggests those long summer evenings when the day is not yet dead, and the night not yet come:

> *Hamm.* Is it light?
> *Clov.* It isn't dark.
> *Hamm* (*angrily*). I'm asking you is it light.
> *Clov.* Yes. (p. 63)

From every point of view, the characters are in a threshold-situation from which there is no escape, for each step can lead only further into the ambiguous world whose prototype, for Beckett, was perhaps Belacqua's purgatory. Asked if he believes in "a life to come," Hamm answers: "Mine was always that" (p. 49); and the play suggests something even worse, that it always will be.

The most pressing problem for people in such a situation is to occupy the enormously distended and slowly growing time in which they live. It can be filled only with actions and words, and in *Endgame,* which is unlike *Waiting for Godot* in this respect, largely with words. But the characters are in a real sense at the end of their tether; they have reached the unending end of a long existence already filled with action and words, so it is not surprising that they should be weary, and especially that they should have run out of inspiration. Unable to find new words, new gestures, they are reduced to repeating indefinitely the things they have already done and said many times

---

the name of the "right" philosopher. He comments on the compulsion this reveals not to divulge more about the play than is included in it; I would add that it shows a desire to protect the *allusiveness* of the text, as being more important than the elucidation of its actual allusions.

before. Their life is not unlike Hamm's story, which he is able to "get on with," "in spite of everything" (p. 59), but which appears at one and the same time to be hopelessly bogged down in repetition and frighteningly near its conclusion:

> *Clov.* Will it not soon be the end?
> *Hamm.* I'm afraid it will.
> *Clov.* Pah! You'll make up another.
> *Hamm.* I don't know. (*Pause.*) I feel rather drained. (p. 61)

This alarm at the prospect of an end is important: Hamm clings to his old story for fear of being left with no story at all. And the characters cling to their repetitious life of gestures and words for similar reasons. One might expect them to look forward to an end which would mark the beginning of a life which would no longer be a mere "story"; but although they dream constantly of this life of silence, motionlessness and repose, they just as constantly betray this ideal through their need for words, movement and action, as though the thought of enormous, *unfilled* time is unbearable to them. Thus they delay their own progress towards an end. Their attitude to life is, consequently, a deeply ambiguous one: they wish to be rid of it, but cannot give it up. Nell puts her finger on it when she remarks that nothing is funnier than unhappiness:

> But it's always the same thing. Yes, it's like the funny story we have heard too often, we still find it funny, but we don't laugh any more. (p. 19)

Of life, as of the "story," it might be said that *nous la trouvons toujours bonne, mais nous n'en rions plus.*

One recognises here something like a weary version of the Pascalian notion of "divertissement"—but the characters think of their life rather in terms of the theater. Hamm, as his name suggests, is an actor, and we have already said that he "represents" what he cannot "be." We may now add that he represents *instead of* being, playing his part in an action which is partly a chess-game (the endgame in chess being that stage when the end is in sight although still in doubt), and partly a play. "Me to play" are his first words, and they are appropriately ambiguous. But the whole of *Endgame* is a kind of image of itself, commenting on itself as a play and thus commenting on life itself as theater. From the curtain-rise of Hamm's awakening (when Clov removes the sheet that covers him) to its fall when at the end of the play he covers his face with his handkerchief (this shrinking is not without its significance, of course), the "action" consists of gestures and words which the characters know are repeated day by day, tiredly, tiresomely, but tirelessly. "Why this farce, day by day?" complains Nell; and ironically, even this is repeated a few moments later by Clov (pp. 14 and 32). "Let's stop playing," Clov implores towards the end (p. 77), but Hamm knows it is not possible, having already explained why:

Clov. What is there to keep me here?
Hamm. The dialogue. (p. 58)

It is difficult indeed to playact alone; one needs an audience, and one needs support. The reason all the characters need one another so desperately is that there must be someone to *donner la réplique,* as the French text puts it. The alternative is solitude and silence, which they desire, but fear as much as they desire it. Someone is necessary to serve as an ear to listen and a mouth to return speech; or even as an eye to look at one, like Hamm's dog, conferring at least that outward existence—the *impression d'exister* Didi and Gogo speak of in *Godot*—which is the only existence one has until one has reached one's central self, but which effectively stands in the way of one's ever reaching that self. So long as, like Hamm, a man needs another to talk about himself (his self?) to, to impose himself on, he is an actor assuming a role, and living not *within* himself but *for* an audience of other people. That is why Hamm allows the others to invade his inner space, and binds them to him as solidly as he is able; but for them, his gestures and words would be meaningless (although, so long as they are present, he can only be gestures and words). Similarly, the others cannot dispense with Hamm:

Hamm. (. . .) Why do you stay with me?
Clov. Why do you keep me?
Hamm. There's no one else.
Clov. There's nowhere else. (p. 6)

Anyone, provided it is someone; anywhere, provided it is somewhere. All are interdependent, like chess-pieces or actors in a play, or like ham(m) and clov(es). A hamm-er is meaningless in a world without nails (cf. Clov-*clou,* Nell-nail, Nagg-*Nagel*),[7] but so too are nails in a world without hammers.

All this is not to stop the hammer from dreaming, however, of another existence, far from nails, a life without gestures or words.

[7] Cf. Hugh Kenner, *op. cit.,* p. 156. [See this volume p. 54.] For other resonances contained in these names see Ruby Cohn, *Samuel Beckett: the Comic Gamut,* New Brunswick (Rutgers University Press, 1962), pp. 219 and 235. [See this volume, pp. 40–52.]

When finally Hamm launches into his "last soliloquy," it is the test of solitude he is facing, and we shall look at the meaning of this ending presently. But a moment or two before he has already attempted to imagine this solitude, and drawn back from it in terror:

> If I can hold my peace, and sit quiet, it will be all over with sound, and motion, all over and done with. (*Pause.*) I'll have called my father and I'll have called my . . . (*he hesitates*) . . . my son. And even twice, or three times, in case they shouldn't have heard me, the first time, or the second. (*Pause.*) I'll say to myself, He'll come back. (*Pause.*) And then? (*Pause.*) And then? (*Pause.*) He couldn't, he has gone too far. (*Pause.*) And then? (*Pause. Very agitated.*) All kinds of fantasies! (pp. 69–70)

Here the dream of silence, motionlessness and independent selfhood is more like a nightmare. Solitude, to Hamm, is a kind of prison, in which one is not even alone: "All kinds of fantasies! That I'm being watched! A rat! Steps!" He recoils from the thought, no more able to take the step away from the world of playacting than he is able to stop breathing—a feat which, alone of Beckett's people, Mr. Endon (= "within"), the suicide by apnoea in *Murphy,* was able to bring off. Hamm continues:

> Breath held and then . . . (*he breathes out.*) Then babble, babble, words, like the solitary child who turns himself into children, two, three, so as to be together, and whisper together, in the dark. (p. 70)

It is not simply the inescapable mechanism of infinitely approaching the infinite, then, which holds us forever on the threshold of our selves; it is also an invisible force—some fear or anguish—concerning which Beckett is extraordinarily discreet, but which I shall call the fear of the void. Over against the conviction of selfhood lies the opposite terror, that at our center is to be found, not a tiny plenum at eternal liberty in the surrounding void, but an inner emptiness at one with the emptiness without, a prison of endless time. That is the fear that has destroyed our calm. When the time comes at last for Hamm to take the sedative (*le calmant*) he has been anxiously calling for since the beginning of the play, he learns a shocking piece of news:

> *Clov.* There's no more pain-killer. (*Pause.*)
> *Hamm* (*appalled*). Good . . . ! (*Pause.*) No more pain-killer!
> *Clov.* No more pain-killer. You'll never get any more pain-killer. (*Pause.*)
> *Hamm.* But the little round box. It was full!
> *Clov.* Yes. But now it's empty. (p. 71)

Humanity has lost its *calmant,* that is the burden of the play, and indeed of all Beckett's work. We have lost our faith in our selves, in our own existence; it seems that the little round box, which once was full, is now empty, like the world itself. Is there then an end for man? And, if that end comes, is it death pure and simple—death and nothing more? Or is the true life of a self at last set free from all that is external to it? Beckett does not answer these questions; he expresses the anxiety.

That is why the conclusion of the play, when Hamm embarks on his monologue and seems at last ready to face solitude, is a masterpiece of ambiguity. When Hamm places the handkerchief over his face and prepares to "sleep," we do not know how the gesture is to be interpreted. Perhaps it means death; or perhaps the repose so long desired; and perhaps the curtain will rise again to-morrow on the unending, repetitive play we have just witnessed. Is the endgame won, lost, or merely "to be continued"? All three possibilities are in line with the suggestions of the text, which excludes none and imposes none of them. We may say that it offers a certainty and a doubt—the certainty that man lives somewhere between an inner and an outer world, belonging fully to neither and partly to both; the doubt which so ambiguous an existence casts on our end. For even the most optimistic conclusion—which would have it that at the center is a timeless, spaceless note of freedom—resolves into inescapable uncertainty, since by definition it makes the approach to selfhood an infinite process, which at once confirms the existence of the self and precludes all hope of attaining it. Everything comes down to the *peut-être* of Clov's opening phrase: *"Fini, c'est fini, ça va finir, ça va peut-être finir,"* and the *must* of the English equivalent slightly alters the stress without changing the problem: "Finished, it's finished, nearly finished, it must be nearly finished." Or perhaps, to return to our point of departure, it all lies in the way one interprets the performance, the *Ausführung* that constitutes the subject and sole reality of *Endgame*. Is our life of words and gestures in time and space—the life we repeat day after day, absurdly, like a play—to be taken as mere words and gestures, a gratuitous agitation in the void? Or is it, also like a play, a representation: a mask, a role, the outer shell of another, inner reality on which it rests and to which it refers, a metaphor or symbol in which the visible and explicit can only point towards an essential being, concealed and problematical, which lies somewhere beyond . . . ever beyond?

Towards an Understanding of *Endgame*

by Theodor W. Adorno

To S. B. in memory of Paris, Fall 1958

Beckett's work bears a certain similarity to Parisian Existentialism. Reminiscences of Absurdity, Situation, Choice (or its contrary), clutter his texts like medieval ruins in Kafka's uncanny town-house; from time to time, the windows fly open to reveal the black, starless sky of something like Anthropology. Yet, if the form of Sartre's fundamentally traditional, thesis-drama is designed primarily to heighten the effect, form in Beckett's work eclipses the message and changes it. The impulses are raised to the level of the most advanced artistic medium, that of Joyce and Kafka. Absurdity for Beckett is no longer diluted to an abstract Idea of Existence, to be illustrated in a Situation. The poetic process abandons itself to absurdity without a guiding intention. Absurdity is stripped of that theoretical generality which, even in Existentialism—the doctrine of the irreducibility of individual existence—is linked to the Western pathos for the Universal and Permanent. Existentialist conformity, the notion that one should *be* what one *is,* with its corollary of a readily understandable style, is rejected. The philosophical tidbits that Beckett serves up are deliberately presented as the refuse of culture, comprising countless allusions and erudition in the tradition of Joyce and Eliot. His work teems with culture, just as Progress, before him, swarmed with the ornaments of *art nouveau:* modernity as the obsolescence of the modern. A regressive language demolishes this tradition. A matter-of-fact attitude in Beckett destroys the rudiments of culture and the meaning it once sought to be. Exposed to this fluoroscope, culture becomes fluorescent. Beckett

---

"Towards an Understanding of Endgame*" by Theodor W. Adorno [Original title: "Versuch das Endspiel zu verstehen"]. From* Noten zur Literatur *II (Frankfurt am Main: Suhrkamp Verlag, 1961; London: Jonathan Cape Limited).* *Translated by Samuel M. Weber. Reprinted by permission of Suhrkamp Verlag, Frankfurt am Main and Jonathan Cape Limited.*

thereby develops a tendency of the modern novel to its final consequence. Reflection, which aesthetic immanence tabooed as too "abstract," is reintroduced, welded together with elements of pure representation; the Flaubertian principle of the pure, self-contained object is undermined. The less tenable the supposition that the events of life are inherently meaningful, the more illusory becomes the conception of aesthetic form as an harmonious unity of appearance and meaning. Beckett rejects this illusion and joins the two precisely in their disharmony. Thought becomes the means by which meaning, inaccessible to direct manifestation, is produced; at the same time it expresses the absence of meaning. Applied to the drama, the word, "meaning," is ambiguous. It covers the metaphysical substance which presents itself objectively in the complexion of the artifact; it designates the significance of the whole, conceived of as being inherently meaningful; and finally, it can signify the meaning of the words and phrases spoken by the characters, including the sequences of dialogue. Yet the ambiguity of these meanings indicates, despite all disparity, a common ground out of which there develops, in *Endgame,* a continuum. The historical basis of this development is a change in the Apriori of drama consisting in the fact that no positive metaphysical meaning is sufficiently substantial any longer—if it ever was—to endow the form of the drama with its own law and epiphany. This loss of meaning, it must be understood, undermines the dramatic form down to the innermost structure of its language. In the face of this dilemma the drama cannot simply react negatively, by grasping the remnants of meaning or its absence and making this its new substance; were it to do so, the effect would be to transform the essence of drama into its opposite. The specificity of drama was traditionally constituted through its metaphysical meaning. If the drama seeks to outlive the demise of this meaning by defining itself as a purely aesthetic form, it necessarily becomes inadequate to its substance and degrades itself to a rattling mechanism for the production of ideological demonstrations, thus becoming the vehicle of abstract notions, as is largely the case of Existentialist drama. The distintegration of metaphysical meaning, which alone assured the unity of the aesthetic structure, destroys the coherence of the traditional dramaturgical canon with the same implacable necessity evident in the general decay of aesthetic forms. An unequivocal aesthetic meaning, subjectified in a solid, tangible intention, would surrogate just that transcendent significance, the denial of which itself provides the substance. Through its own organization of senselessness, the plot is forced to fashion itself after that which originally constituted the truth of the dramatic dimension as such. This construction of the senseless affects even the molecules of language: if they and their constellations become rationally significant, they will inevitably synthesize into just that coherent meaning which the whole denies. Hence, the interpretation of *Endgame* cannot pursue the chimera of expressing the play's meaning through philosophical mediation. Understanding *Endgame* can only be understanding why it cannot be understood, concretely reconstructing the coherent meaning of its incoherence. Thought, isolated in the drama, no longer pretends, as the Idea once did, to exhaust the meaning of the work, or to converge with the transcendence traditionally generated and guaranteed by aesthetic immanence. Instead, it transforms itself into a kind of second-degree material, like the philosophizing in Thomas Mann's *Magic Mountain* and *Doctor Faustus,* which is itself developed as material, replacing the tangible immediacy increasingly excluded from the self-conscious work of art. If this materiality of thought was hitherto largely unintentional, the dilemma of works which confused themselves with the idea they were incapable of attaining, Beckett faces up to the challenge and employs thoughts, *sans phrase,* as clichés, elements of the *monologue intérieur* to which the mind itself has been reduced, by the reified regression of culture. If Existentialism prior to Beckett degraded philosophy to the level of a poetic project—thus reincarnating Schiller—Beckett, more cultivated than all the others, presents it with the bill: philosophy, the mind itself, proclaims its own worthlessness, dreamlike dross of the empirical world, while the poetic process declares itself a waste. *Dégout,* since Baudelaire artistically productive, becomes insatiable in Beckett's historically mediated impulses. Everything which is no longer valid crystallizes into a canon, thus redeeming a motif dating from the prehistory of Existentialism, Husserl's universal annihilation of the world, which is wrenched from the shadow-realm of methodology. Totalitarians like Lukács, who rage against the "decadence" of Beckett's truly terrifying simplifications, are not wholly unjustified from the standpoint of their masters. They detest in Beckett what they themselves have betrayed. Only the nausea of surfeit, the tedium of the mind's own "purity," can desire that which would be wholly different; prescribed health, on the contrary, prefers the available nourishment, plain fare. Beckett's *dégout* does not permit itself to be coerced. Invited to pitch in, it responds with parody, both of the philosophy spewed forth in the dialogues, and of the forms themselves. Existentialism itself is parodied; nothing is left of its invariants, refurbished *vérités éternelles,* but bare existence. The opposition of the drama to ontology —the system of the First and Permanent (no matter of what kind)— becomes unmistakable when the dialogue unintentionally parodies

Goethe's saying about the good old truths, *das alte Wahre,* a notion whose fate was to degenerate into a bourgeois mentality:

> *Hamm.* Do you remember your father?
> *Clov* (*wearily*). Same answer. (*Pause.*) You've asked me these questions millions of times.
> *Hamm.* I love the old questions. (*With fervour.*) Ah the old questions, the old answers, there's nothing like them! (*Endgame,* Grove Press, 38)

Thoughts are dragged along and distorted like vestiges of experience in dreams, *homo homini sapienti sat.* Hence, the dubiousness of that with which Beckett refuses to concern himself: his interpretation. He shrugs at the possibility of philosophy today, at that of theory in general. The irrationality of bourgeois society in its advanced phase resists comprehension; those were the good old days when a critique of the political economy of this society could be written by taking it at its own *ratio.* In the meanwhile, society has thrown its *ratio* into the dustbin and replaced it with direct control. The interpreting word thus inevitably falls short of Beckett, although his dramas, precisely by virtue of being restricted to isolated, abstract facticity, twitch convulsively beyond mere facts and enigmatically demand interpretation. The ability to deal with this enigma might well be the criterion of philosophy today.

French Existentialism sought to come to grips with history. With Beckett, history devours Existentialism. In *Endgame,* a historical moment unfolds: the experience crystallized in the title of a best-seller of the Culture Industry: *Kaputt.* After the Second World War, everything, including a resurrected culture, was destroyed, although without its knowledge. In the wake of events which even the survivors cannot survive, mankind vegetates, crawling forward on a pile of rubble, denied even the awareness of its own ruin. This state of affairs is snatched from the clutches of the market, the pragmatic precondition of the play:

> *Clov* (*He gets up on ladder, turns the telescope on the without.*) Let's see. (*He looks, moving the telescope.*) Zero . . . (*he looks*) . . . zero . . . (*he looks*) . . . and zero.
> *Hamm.* Nothing stirs. All is—
> *Clov.* Zer—
> *Hamm* (*violently*). Wait till you're spoken to! (*Normal voice.*) All is . . . all is . . . all is what? (*Violently.*) All is what?
> *Clov.* What all is? In a word? Is that what you want to know? Just a moment. (*He turns the telescope on the without, lowers the telescope, turns towards Hamm.*) Corpsed. (29–30)

The fact that all human beings are dead is smuggled in with sleight of hand. An earlier passage suggests why the catastrophe must not be mentioned. Hamm himself is somehow responsible:

Hamm. That old doctor, he's dead, naturally?
Clov. He wasn't old.
Hamm. But he's dead?
Clov. Naturally. (*Pause.*) *You* ask *me* that? (24–25)

The play's setting, however, is none other than the earth upon which "there's no more nature" (11). The phase in which the world is totally reified, in which nothing is left that is not made by man, the permanent catastrophe, becomes indistinguishable from a supplementary, man-made catastrophe, in which nature is destroyed and after which nothing grows any longer:

Hamm. Did your seeds come up?
Clov. No.
Hamm. Did you scratch round them to see if they had sprouted?
Clov. They haven't sprouted.
Hamm. Perhaps it's still too early.
Clov. If they were going to sprout they would have sprouted. (*Violently.*) They'll never sprout. (13)

The *dramatis personae* resemble persons dreaming of their own death, in a shelter where, nevertheless, "it's time it ended." (3) The end of the world is discounted as though it were self-evident. Every aspiring drama of the atomic age must become a self-mockery if only because its story reassuringly falsifies the historical horror of anonymity by introducing characters and human action, and perhaps even succumbs to an adulation of the "leaders" who decide whether or not the button will be pressed. The violence of the unutterable is mimed by the dread of mentioning it. Beckett keeps it nebulous. That which is incommensurable to all experience can only be spoken of in euphemisms, the way people in Germany speak of the murder of the Jews. It has become the total Apriori, leaving a bombed-out consciousness no place from which it could meditate. This desperate state of affairs provides, with grisly irony, a stylistic technique which protects this pragmatic precondition from being contaminated by infantile science fiction. Even if Clov did exaggerate, as claimed by his nagging, commonsensical companion, it would not make much difference. The *partial* end of the world, to which the catastrophe would then amount, is a bad joke; nature, from which the prisoners have already taken leave, would be as good as gone; whatever remains would only prolong the agony.

Yet this historical *notabene,* the parody of Kierkegaard's convergence of time and eternity, places a taboo upon history. What Existentialist jargon terms the *condition humaine* crystallizes in the image of the last man devouring his predecessors, mankind. Existential ontology asserts universal validities obtained through a process of abstraction of which it itself is unaware. While still heeding the dictates of the old phenomenological thesis of the eidetic intuition, the *Wesenschau,*—as though the essential determinations manifested themselves in the Particulars, thus magically fusing Apriority and Concretion—ontology in fact only obtains its eternal verities through a process of distillation which annuls the very particularities, the spatial-temporal process of individualization, which makes Existence existence and not merely another concept. Modern ontology thus appeals to those who are weary of philosophical formalism and who nonetheless cling to that which can only be had as form. Beckett confronts this unconscious abstraction with its incisive antithesis: conscious subtraction. Instead of excluding the temporal from existence, which only is existence through its temporality, he subtracts that which time —the historical trend—is in reality preparing to annul. He extends the trajectory of the subject's liquidation to the point where it shrinks to the here-and-now, the abstractness of which, consisting in the loss of all quality, reduces ontology literally *ad absurdum,* to that absurdity which existence becomes once it has dissolved into mere identity. Childish inanity emerges as the substance of a philosophy which has degenerated to a tautology, to the conceptual duplication of the existence it had once set out to comprehend. If modern ontology thrives upon the unfulfilled promise of abstractions which claim to be concrete, Beckett reveals the concretism of a molluscoid existence, withdrawn into itself and incapable of all generality, to be the same as the abstractism which can never attain the level of experience. Ontology is welcomed home as the pathogenesis of a false life. It is represented as the state of negative eternity. If the messianic Myshkin once forgot his watch because mundane time was irrelevant to him, time is lost to his antipodes because it might signify hope. The bored confirmation that the weather is "the same as usual," (4) opens the inferno:

> *Hamm.* But that's always the way at the end of the day, isn't it, Clov?
> *Clov.* Always.
> *Hamm.* It's the end of the day like any other day, isn't it, Clov?
> *Clov.* Looks like it. (13)

Like time itself, the temporal is disabled; to say that it no longer existed would be too much of a consolation. It is and is not, like the world for the Solipsist, who doubts its existence while conceding it with every word. Thus, at one point, the dialogue hovers:

Hamm. And the horizon? Nothing on the horizon?
Clov (*lowering the telescope, turning towards Hamm, exasperated*). What in God's name could there be on the horizon? (*Pause.*)
Hamm. The waves, how are the waves?
Clov. The waves? (*He turns the telescope on the waves.*) Lead.
Hamm. And the sun?
Clov (*looking*). Zero.
Hamm. But it should be sinking. Look again.
Clov (*looking*). Damn the sun.
Hamm. Is it night already then?
Clov (*looking*). No.
Hamm. Then what is it?
Clov (*looking*). Gray. (*Lowering the telescope, turning towards Hamm, louder.*) Gray! (*Pause. Still louder.*) GRRAY! (31)

History is excluded because it has dried up the power of consciousness to conceive history: the power of memory. Drama loses its voice and becomes gesture, freezing in the middle of dialogues. All that appears of history is its result, its decline. What for the Existentialists inflated itself into the once-and-for-all of Being-there, *Dasein,* shrinks to the end-point of history and breaks off. Lukács, who attacks Beckett for reducing human beings to their animality,[1] rejects, with official optimism, the fact that the residual philosophies, which credit themselves with the True and Immutable after subtracting all temporal contingencies, have themselves become the residue of life, the sum total of ruin. However wrong it is to attribute an abstract, subjectivistic ontology to Beckett as Lukács does, it would be no less so to cite him as a political star-witness. The struggle against atomic annihilation will find little encouragement in a work which traces the aggressive potential back to the most ancient struggle of all. The simplifier of terror, in contrast to Brecht, refuses all simplification. He is, however, not so unlike Brecht inasmuch as his capacity for differentiation becomes an allergy to subjective differences that have degenerated to the conspicuous consumption of those who could afford the luxury of individuation. This reflects a social truth. Differentiation cannot be credited, sight unseen, as a positive process. The simplification of the current process of socialization relegates it to the *faux frais,* the superfluous expenses, a fate similar to that which befell the social

[1] Cf. Th. W. Adorno, "Expresste Versöhnung," *Noten zur Literatur II* (Frankfurt am Main, 1961), p. 166, and Georg Lukács, *Wider den missverstandenen Realismus* (Hamburg, 1958), p. 31.

amenities, whose disappearance took with it the capacity to differentiate which they once rendered possible. Differentiation, once the condition of humanity, gradually becomes ideology. Yet the unsentimental awareness of this fact is not itself regressive. In the act of omission the omitted survives as that which has been avoided, like consonance in atonal harmony. The primitiveness of *Endgame* is registered and observed with the greatest differentiation. The unprotesting presentation of ubiquitous regression protests against a world-order which so totally heeds the law of regression that it has virtually lost every alternative action which might have opposed this trend. In *Endgame,* strictest surveillance assures that all things remain as they are, that nothing different is permitted; a highly sensitive alarm system determines what fits into the topography of the play and filters out what has no place there. Gentleness leads Beckett to shun the gentle as well as the brutal. The vanity of the individual who accuses society while at the same time his own "rights" help contribute to the general calamity, to the injustice affecting all individuals, manifests itself in embarrassing declamations like the "Deutschland" poem of Karl Wolfskehl. Too late, having missed the historical moment, such bursts of rhetoric are condemned to be empty phrases. Nothing of the kind in Beckett. Even the conception which negatively represents the negativity of the epoch, accommodates the attitude prevalent in the Eastern satellites, where the task of art is defined as the healthy and vigorous reflection of a healthy and vigorous epoch. Divested of all intention to mirror reality, Beckett's drama plays with its elements, takes no position and seeks its luck in the "liberty" of a bureaucratized existence; yet in the process it reveals far more than could the revelations of any party. Only in silence can the name of the catastrophe be pronounced. The horror of the whole explodes in the latest calamity, not in the search for origins. Man, whose generic name is out of place in the landscape of Beckett's language, is for him strictly what he has become. Decisive for the species is its last day, the day of judgment, as in utopia. Yet in the mind even the lament of this end must reflect upon the fact that there is nothing left to be lamented. No tears melt the armor; all that is left is the face whose tears have run dry. This is the basis of an artistic stance denounced as inhuman by those whose humanity has already become propaganda for the inhuman, even where the propagandists themselves are unaware of the change. The fear of such blindness is probably the innermost motivation of Beckett's reduction of man to animality. Part of the absurd in his work is that it veils its own features.

The catastrophes which are the inspiration of *Endgame* have exploded the individual, whose substantiality and absoluteness provided the common ground for Kierkegaard, Jaspers and the Sartrean version of Existentialism. The latter went so far as to endow the victim of the concentration camp with the liberty of inwardly accepting or rejecting the martyrdom imposed upon him from without. *Endgame* destroys such illusions. The individual, both the result of the capitalist process of alienation and the stubborn protest against it, reveals its ephemeral character as an historical category. The individualistic position stands in polar but necessary relation to the ontological orientation of all Existentialism including that of *Being and Time*. Beckett's drama deserts this position like an outmoded bunker. There is no justification for the claim of individual experience, in its narrow and contingent dimension, to interpret itself as a figure of Being, unless it asserts itself to be the fundamental character of Being. Yet precisely this is untrue. The immediacy of individuation is illusory; that to which individual human experience clings is itself mediated, conditioned. *Endgame* takes for granted that the claims of the individual to possess autonomy and ontological status have become implausible. But while the prison of individuation is exposed both as a prison and an illusion—the image of such self-reflection is the scene of *Endgame*—art is incapable of breaking the spell of isolated subjectivity; all it can do is to depict the solipsism. Beckett thus collides with the antinomy of modern art. The position of the Absolute Subject, once cracked open as the manifestation of the transcendent whole which engendered it, can no longer be defended. Expressionism becomes obsolete. Yet the passage to the valid universality of an objective reality, which would end the semblance of individuation, is blocked to art. Unlike the discursive cognition of reality, from which art is distinguished not gradually but categorically, aesthetic validity is restricted to that which can be assimilated at the level of subjectivity, and which must therefore be commensurable to it. Reconciliation, the supreme idea of art, can only be conceived as that between the estranged. For art to feign reconciliation by defecting to the world of things, would be for it to negate itself. What is offered under the name of Socialist Realism does not surpass subjectivism but falls short of it and is at the same time its pre-artistic complement; Expressionist pathos and ideologically seasoned social reportage go together. Unreconciled reality does not tolerate reconciliation with the object in art; realism which does not even reach the level of subjective experience, much less surpass it, is merely the mimicry of reality. The dignity of art today depends not upon whether it manages, through skill or luck, to skirt this antinomy, but rather on the fashion in which it articulates it. In this respect *Endgame* is exemplary. It yields both to the fact that works of art can no longer depict and process materials as in the nineteenth century, and to the insight that the subjective modes of reaction which have replaced simple depiction as the medium of artistic form are themselves neither primary nor absolute but derived, objectively produced. The entire substance of a subjectivity which necessarily hypostasizes itself is the trace and shadow of the world from which it withdraws in order not to succumb to the illusion and adjustment demanded by that world. Beckett responds to this not by posing an inalienable reserve but by citing the very fragility which the antagonistic tendencies still permit, albeit precariously and subject to constant revocation. His drama recalls the jest, popular years ago in Germany, of cavorting about between the border posts of Baden and Bavaria as though they staked out a realm of freedom. *Endgame* takes place in a zone of indifference, between interiority and exteriority, neutral both towards the materials without which no subjectivity can express itself or even be, and towards an élan which blurs all things as though its breath steamed up the glass through which they are viewed. The materials are so scanty that aesthetic formalism is ironically saved from its adversaries in both camps: the hacks of dialectical materialism as well as the connoisseurs of authentic statement. The concretism of Beckett's lemures, whose horizon has been lost in a double sense, metamorphoses directly into the most extreme abstraction; the material dimension itself inaugurates a process through which the materials (reduced to the vanishing point) begin to resemble geometric forms: the most limited become the most general. By situating *Endgame* in such a zone, its readers are teased by a suggestion of symbolism which Beckett, no less than Kafka, rejects. Because nothing is simply that which it is, everything seems to be a sign of something inward; yet the implicit inward referent no longer exists, and that is precisely the significance of the signs. The minimum ration of reality and characters with which the drama must make ends meet is identical with the vestiges of subject, mind and soul which survive the permanent catastrophe. Of the mind, which originated in mimesis, there remains ludicrous imitation; the stage-struck soul survives as inhuman sentimentality; and the subject, which exists only in its most abstract form, being-there, becomes a mockery of itself. Beckett's figures behave in such a primitively behavioristic manner that only the circumstances ensuing after the total catastrophe suffice to render them comprehensible; they have been so mutilated by the catastrophe that the only reaction of which they are still capable is that of flies, twitching after having been half squashed by the swatter. The aesthetic principles of stylization does the same to human beings. The subjects, entirely thrown back upon themselves, incarnations of acosmism, consist of nothing but the impoverished realities of a world which has shrunk to bare necessity;

as empty personae they have truly become mere sounding-boards. Their phonyness is the result of a process of demystification which reveals the Spirit to be a myth. In order to underbid history and thus perhaps to survive it, *Endgame* occupies the nadir of what, at the zenith of philosophy was appropriated by the construction of the Subject-Object: pure identity, which here becomes that of the victimized, of subject and object in the state of utter estrangement. If Kafka's meanings were beheaded or obscure, Beckett puts an end to interminable intentionality which seeks to claim that meaninglessness itself is meaningful. This is objectively, devoid of all polemical intent, his response to Existentialism, which had sought, first through its concept of "thrownness," and then of "absurdity," to transfigure meaninglessness into meaning by exploiting the ambiguity inherent in the notion of meaning. Beckett does not endeavor to replace Existentialism with an alternative world-view: he simply takes it at its word. What remains of absurdity once the meaning of existence has been cut down to size is no longer a universal—that would simply make the absurd into an idea—but rather dismal details which scorn conceptualization, a region filled with utensils, suggesting emergency quarters, refrigerators, paralysis, blindness and unappetizing bodily functions. Everything waits to be carted off—to the dump, or to the death camps. This region is not symbolic but rather the state of affairs in which psychology is no longer relevant: that of the aged and the tortured.

Heidegger's States of Mind (*Befindlichkeiten*), Jasper's Situations are dragged from the sphere of inwardness and materialized. In both systems the hypostasis of the individual and that of the situation betray a complicity. Situation came to designate temporal existence as such, and the living individual in its totality was considered to be that which is absolutely certain. Both notions presupposed personal identity. Beckett, however, shows himself to be the pupil of Joyce and friend of Proust by restoring to the notion of situation its explicit meaning, which had been methodically obscured by the philosophy which thus sought to exploit it. By dissociating the unity of consciousness into its disparate elements, Beckett reaffirms its nonidentity. However, once the identity of the subject is no longer taken for granted, the distinction between the outer world and inner situations becomes fluid and those situations must be seen as themselves pertaining to nature. The verdict which condemns individuality condemns idealism as well, and thus the idealistic nucleus conserved in Existentialism. Nonidentity comprises both of these elements: the historical disintegration of the subject as a unity, and the emergence of that which is not subject. This alters the meaning of situation. Jaspers has defined it as "a reality for a subject interested in it as existence." [2] He subordinates the notion of situation to that of the subject, conceived as being stable and identical, just as he assumes that the situation becomes meaningful through its relation to this subject. Immediately thereafter he speaks of the situation as "a reality which is not merely natural, but significant (*sinnbezogen*)"; this "significance," he alleges, remarkably enough, is "neither psychic nor physical but both at once." [3] When, however, the situation in Beckett's work really becomes "both at once," it loses its existential-ontological constituents: personal identity and meaning. This becomes *éclatant* in the notion of the *Grenzsituation,* the Borderline Situation. It, too, stems from Jaspers: "Situations such as the fact that I am always in situations, that I cannot live with struggle and without suffering, that I ineluctably assume guilt, that I must die, these I call borderline situations. They never change, except in their manifestations; in relation to our existence, they are of ultimate validity." [4] *Endgame*'s construction responds to this with a dry, "I beg your pardon?" Platitudes such as "I cannot live without suffering, that I ineluctably assume guilt, that I must die," lose their banality as soon as they are hauled back down from their sublime Apriority into the world of appearances. The noble, affirmative veneer with which philosophy adorns what Hegel once called a "rotten existence" is thus stripped away: the sleight-of-hand by which the nonconceptual is subsumed under a concept—thus eliminating precisely what modern ontology has pompously named "Difference"—is here mercilessly exposed. Beckett stands Existential philosophy on its feet. His play is a reaction to the comedy and ideological aberration of phrases like: "In borderline situations, bravery is the attitude towards death as the indeterminate possibility of being oneself." [5] This response is objective, whether or not it was intended by the author. The poverty of the players in *Endgame* is that of philosophy.

Beckett's situations, out of which the drama is composed, are the negations of significant reality. They are modelled upon those of empirical existence, which, once isolated, torn from their pragmatic and psychological context through the loss of personal unity, spontaneously assume a specific, compelling visage: that of sheer horror. They are already to be found in the praxis of Expressionism. The horrifying aspect of Leonhard Frank's teacher, Mager, which is ulti-

[2] Jaspers, *Philosophie* (Berlin-Göttingen-Heidelberg, 1956), Vol. 2, p. 201 f.

[3] *Ibid.*, p. 202.

[4] *Ibid.*, p. 203.

[5] Heinrich Rickert, *Unmittelbarkeit und Sinndeutung* (Tübingen, 1939), p. 133 f.

mately responsible for his murder, becomes manifest in the description of the elaborate manner in which Herr Mager peels an apple in front of his class. The deliberateness, apparently so innocent, is the figure of sadism: the image of someone taking his time suggests the torturer who lets his victims wait for him. Beckett's use of situations, the terrifying, artificial offspring of simple-minded "situation" comedy, helps to articulate a state of things which had previously been observed in Proust. In his posthumous work, *Immediacy and Interpretation,* the Neo-Kantian philosopher, Heinrich Rickert, discusses the possibility of an objective physiognomy of the spirit, a physiognomy which would be more than the merely "projective" "soul" of a landscape or of a work of art. In this context, he cites a passage in which Ernst Robert Curtius discusses Proust. Curtius argues that it is

> only in part correct . . . to regard Proust exclusively or predominantly as a great psychologist. A Stendhal is adequately characterized by this term. He . . . thus stands in the Cartesian tradition of the French spirit. But Proust refuses to recognize the separation between thinking and extended substance. He does not divide the world into psychic and physical dimensions. To view his work from the perspective of the "psychological novel" is to misunderstand its meaning. The world of sensible things is no less important in Proust's work than that of the mind.

Or: "If Proust is a psychologist, it is in an entirely novel sense: submerging everything real, including sensible intuition, in a mental flux." "The ordinary notion of the psychic is not adequate here," Rickert comments, again citing Curtius: "The notion of the psychological has thus lost its opposite—and precisely for this reason is no longer a suitable characterization." [6] The physiognomy of objective expression retains nonetheless an enigmatic moment. The situations say something—but what? Here art itself, as the quintessence of situations, converges with physiognomy. Art unites the greatest delineation with its radical opposite. In Beckett the contradiction is turned inside-out. What ordinarily hides behind the facade of communication is dragged out into the open. Proust clings affirmatively to physiognomy, thus continuing a subterranean mystical tradition, as though involuntary memory were to reveal a secret language of things. In Beckett this becomes the language of the no-longer-human. His situations are the counter-images of the indelible moments evoked in Proust's work, snatched from the tide of what panic-stricken health seeks to drown out with its cries of bloody murder: schizophrenia. Descending into

[6] Ernst Robert Curtius, *Französischer Geist im neuen Europa* (1925), p. 74 ff., cited by Heinrich Rickert, *ibid.,* p. 133 ff., footnote.

its realm, Beckett's drama still retains its control. It even manages to reflect:

> *Hamm.* I once knew a madman who thought the end of the world had come. He was a painter—and engraver. I had a great fondness for him. I used to go and see him, in the asylum. I'd take him by the hand and drag him to the window. Look! There! All that rising corn! And there! Look! The sails of the herring fleet! All that loveliness! (*Pause.*) He'd snatch away his hand and go back into his corner. Appalled. All he had seen was ashes. (*Pause.*) He alone had been spared. (*Pause.*) Forgotten. (*Pause.*) It appears the case is . . . was not so . . . so unusual. (44)

The madman's perception is that of Clov, peering out of the window upon command. *Endgame* moves away from the nadir solely by chanting to itself, like a sleepwalker, "negation of negativity." Lodged in Beckett's memory is something like the picture of an apoplectic, middle-aged man taking his afternoon nap, with a towel over his eyes to shield him from the flies and the light: it makes him unrecognizable. The commonplace image, familiar enough visually, only becomes a sign for the observer who is sensitive to the loss of identity of the face, to the possibility that its veil could cover a corpse, to the repugnance of physical suffering which, by reducing the living to his body, already includes him among the dead.[7] Beckett scrutinizes such aspects until the everyday family life from which they stem pales to irrelevance. In the beginning there is the image of Hamm covered with an old sheet; at the end, he draws the handkerchief, his last possession, to his face:

> *Hamm.* Old Stancher! (*Pause.*) You . . . remain. (84)

Situations, thus emancipated from their context and from the characters, are constructed into a second, autonomous context, similar to music which joins its submerged intentions and expressive characteristics until their sequence forms a structure in its own right. A key passage in the play—

> If I can hold my peace, and sit quiet, it will be all over with sound, and motion, all over and done with. (69)

—betrays the underlying principle, in a reminiscence perhaps of Shakespeare's method in the players' scene from *Hamlet*:

[7] Cf. Max Horkheimer and Th. W. Adorno, *Dialektik der Aufklärung* (Amsterdam, 1947), p. 279.

Hamm. Then babble, babble, words, like the solitary child who turns himself into children, two, three, so as to be together, and whisper together, in the dark. (*Pause.*) Moment upon moment, pattering down, like the millet grains of . . . (*he hesitates*) . . . that old Greek, and all life long you wait for that to mount up to a life. (70)

By means of the panic of not being in a hurry, such situations hint at the irrelevance and superfluity of everything the subject can still do. After considering the possibility of screwing down the lids of the trashcans in which his parents live, Hamm revokes his decision to do it with the same words he uses after debating whether or not to urinate and thus to submit himself to the torture of the catheter:

Hamm. Time enough. (24)

The slight revulsion at medicine bottles, dating from the moment when one first became aware of the physical frailty, mortality, decomposition of one's parents, comes to light once again in the question:

Hamm. Is it not time for my pain-killer? (12)

Speaking with one another has become Strindbergian nagging:

Hamm. You feel normal?
Clov (*irritably*). I tell you I don't complain! (4)

And, another time:

Hamm. I feel a little too far to the left. (*Clov moves chair slightly.*) Now I feel a little too far to the right. (*Clov moves chair slightly.*) I feel a little too far forward. (*Clov moves chair slightly.*) Now I feel a little too far back. (*Clove moves chair slightly.*) Don't stay there, (*i.e. behind the chair*) you give me the shivers. (*Clov returns to his place beside the chair.*)
Clov. If I could kill him I'd die happy. (27)

The last days of marriage, however, bring the situation of scratching oneself:

Nell. I am going to leave you.
Nagg. Could you give me a scratch before you go?
Nell. No. (*Pause.*) Where?
Nagg. In the back.
Nell. No. (*Pause.*) Rub yourself against the rim.
Nagg. It's lower down. In the hollow.
Nell. What hollow?
Nagg. The hollow! (*Pause.*) Could you not? (*Pause.*) Yesterday you scratched me there.

Nell (*elegiac*). Ah yesterday!
Nagg. Could you not? (*Pause.*) Would you like me to scratch you? (*Pause.*) Are you crying again?
Nell. I was trying. (19–20)

After the abdicated father and preceptor has told his parents the celebrated "metaphysical" Jewish joke about the trousers and the world, he himself bursts out laughing.[8] The shame that one feels when someone laughs at his own words becomes Existential. Life has become the quintessence of all those things about which one ought to feel ashamed. Despotic subjectivity becomes mortifying in a situation where the master whistles and the servant comes running. That against which shame protests, however, has its social significance: When he reveals his true colors, the bourgeois individual degrades the notion of humanity upon which his own pretensions rest. Here, again, Beckett's archetypal images are historical: what is "typically human" are the deformations inflicted upon human beings by the form of their society. No room is left for anything else. The aberrations and ticks of the "normal" personality, intensified in *Endgame* beyond all expectation, characterize all classes and individuals and constitute the universality of a whole that only manages to reproduce itself through the pernicious particularity and the antagonistic interests of its subjects. Yet, because there was no life other than that which was false, the catalogue of its defects becomes the counterpart of ontology.

The fragmentation into the disassociated and unidentical is nonetheless inextricably bound up with the principle of identity in a play which does not renounce the traditional cast of characters. Dissociation as such is only meaningful in opposition to identity and thus falls under the scope of this concept; otherwise, it would simply be pure, unpolemical, innocent multiplicity. The historical crisis of the individual has, for the time being, its limit in the biological individual, which is its scene and setting. Thus, the changing flow of situations in Beckett, meeting no resistance on the part of individuals, ends only with the stubbornness of their bodies, to which they have regressed. Measured against this unity, the schizoid situations become as comic as optical illusions. Thus the clownery evident in the behavior of Beckett's figures, and in the constellations they form.[9] Psychoanalysis explains clownery as a regression to an extremely early ontogenetic level, and Beckett's regression-play descends to such

[8] [Adorno here mistakenly attributes to Hamm the joke which Nagg tells Nell—ED.]

[9] Cf. Günther Anders, *Die Antiquiertheit des Menschen* (Munich, 1956), p. 217.

depths. But the laughter that it evokes ought to choke on itself. This is what has become of humor after it has grown obsolete as an aesthetic medium and revolting without a canon of the truly humorous, without a place of reconciliation from where one could laugh, without anything left between heaven and earth that is really harmless, that would permit itself to be laughed at. An intentionally moronic pun on the weather testifies to this:

> *Clov.* Things are livening up. (*He gets up on ladder, raises the telescope, lets it fall.*) I did it on purpose. (*He gets down, picks up the telescope, turns it on auditorium.*) I see . . . a multitude . . . in transport . . . of joy. (*Pause.*) That's what I call a magnifier. (*He lowers the telescope, turns towards Hamm.*) Well? Don't we laugh? (29)

Humor itself has become inane, ludicrous—who could still laugh at such basic comic texts like *Don Quixote* or *Gargantua*—and Beckett draws the consequences. Even the jokes of the injured are injured. They no longer reach anyone; the degenerate form of humor, the pun —something of which resides in every joke—covers them like leprosy. If Clov, peering through his telescope, is asked about the color he sees and then terrifies Hamm with the word, "gray," he then corrects himself with the formulation, "light black" (32). This smears the *pointe* from Molière's *Miser,* who describes the allegedly stolen chest as greyish red. Wit, like color, is drained dry. At one point the two non-heroes, a blind man and a cripple—the stronger already both, the weaker well on the way—ponder a trick, an escape, "any kind of plan," à la *Threepenny Opera,* about which they do not know whether it will only prolong their lives and agony or end both in absolute annihilation:

> *Clov.* Ah good. (*He starts pacing to and fro, his eyes fixed on the ground, his hands behind his back. He halts.*) The pains in my legs! It's unbelievable! Soon I won't be able to think any more.
>
> *Hamm.* You won't be able to leave me. (*Clov resumes his pacing.*) What are you doing?
>
> *Clov.* Having an idea. (*He paces.*) Ah! (*He halts.*)
>
> *Hamm.* What a brain! (*Pause.*) Well?
>
> *Clov.* Wait! (*He meditates. Not very convinced.*) Yes . . . (*Pause. More convinced.*) Yes! (*He raises his head.*) I have it! I set the alarm. (46–47)

This, too, is presumably an allusion to the Jewish joke of the Busch Circus, which tells of dumb August, who, having caught his wife and his friend on the sofa, cannot decide which one to throw out since both are too dear to him; he finally decides to sell the sofa. Yet even the last trace of inane, sophistic rationality is wiped away by Beckett. All that remains of comedy is the fact that the demise of the punch-line is the demise of comedy itself. Thus, having climbed the last step of the stairs, one shudders, climbs on and steps off into the void. The most extreme brutality carries out the verdict condemning laughter, which has long shared in its guilt. Hamm lets the caracasses of his parents, who have become infants in the trashcans, starve—triumph of the son as father. This to the background music of chatter:

Nagg. Me pap!
Hamm. Accursed progenitor!
Nagg. Me pap!
Hamm. The old folks at home! No decency left! Guzzle, guzzle, that's all they think of. (*He whistles. Enter Clov. He halts beside the chair.*) Well! I thought you were leaving me.
Clov. Oh not just yet, not just yet.
Nagg. Me pap!
Hamm. Give him his pap.
Clov. There's no more pap.
Hamm (*to Nagg*). Do you hear that? There's no more pap. You'll never get any more pap. (9)

The non-hero adds scorn to the irrevocable damage, he fumes at the old people who have no decency left, just as the elderly chastise the young for their immorality. The meagre remnants of humanity in this ambiance, the fact that the two old people share their last biscuit, becomes repugnant by contrast to the transcendental bestiality, the regression of love to drooling infancy. Insofar as they are still human, there are human "touches":

Nell. What is it, my pet? (*Pause.*) Time for love?
Nagg. Were you asleep?
Nell. Oh no!
Nagg. Kiss me!
Nell. We can't.
Nagg. Try. (*Their heads strain towards each other, fail to meet, fall apart again.*) (14)

Not just humor but all the dramatic categories are juggled. All are parodied. Yet not scorned. Parody, in the emphatic sense, is the employment of forms at times when they have become historically impossible. Parody demonstrates this impossibility and thus alters the forms. The three Aristotelian unities are preserved, but the drama itself fights for its life. The drama is deprived of subjectivity, of which

Endgame is the epilogue, and with it, of the possibility of a hero; all that remains of freedom is the impotent and ridiculous reflex of empty decisions.[10] In this respect, as well, Beckett's play is heir to the novels of Kafka, to whom he stands in a similar relation to that of the serial composers to Schoenberg: he reflects Kafka once again in his work and turns him inside-out by totalizing his principle. Beckett's critique of his predecessor, which irrefutably demonstrates the divergence between the action and an objectively pure, epic language, harbors the same difficulty as is encountered by contemporary integral composition in its relation to Schoenberg's inherently antagonistic work. What is the raison d'être of forms once the tension between form and non-form is eliminated as a result of the irresistible progression by which art dominates and assimilates its materials? *Endgame* avoids the antinomy by appropriating the question and making it thematic. That which excludes the dramatization of Kafka's novels becomes itself the guiding principle of the drama. The dramatic constituents appear after their death. Exposition, intrigue, action, peripeteia and catastrophe return as decomposed participants in a dramatical inquest: the catastrophe is replaced by the announcement that there is no more pain-killer (71). These constituents are overthrown together with the meaning into which the drama once sought to crystallize. Contemporary drama, which no longer tolerates the conditions of its own existence, is placed in a test tube in *Endgame* and studied. An example: at the height of the action in tragedy, stichomythy was used as the quintessence of antithesis, producing the most extreme tension in the dramatic fibre through dialogues in which the trimeter of one speaker follows that of another. The form abandoned this technique as being too remote from secular society by virtue of its extreme and overt rhetorical quality. Beckett employs this device as though the detonation had liberated that which the drama had buried. *Endgame* contains dialogues in rapid sequence, monosyllabic like the question-and-answer game between the deluded monarch and the messenger of fate. Yet, while this traditionally served to tighten the development, it slackens it now. Gasping, barely able to speak, the interlocutors are no longer able to reach the synthesis of grammatical phrases and instead stammer a kind of shorthand: whether that of positivism or expressionism is left unclear. The limit-value of Beckett's drama is the silence which, as early as Shakespeare, the origin of the modern tragic drama, was defined as that which remains: the rest. The fact that an *Act without Words* follows *Endgame* as a sort of epilogue, indicates the *terminus ad quem*. The

[10] Cf. Th. W. Adorno, "Notes on Kafka," *Prisms* (London, 1967), pp. 262–63, footnote.

words have a makeshift sound because the silence was not wholly attained; they are the accompaniment to a stillness they disturb.

What has become of form in *Endgame* can virtually be traced in literary history. In Ibsen's *Wild Duck,* the delapidated photographer, Hjalmar Ekdal, already himself a potential non-hero, forgets his promise to bring the adolescent girl, Hedwig, the menu from the lavish dinner at old Werle's house, where he had been invited, without his family. This is psychologically motivated by his slovenly, egoistic personality, yet at the same time it is also symbolic for Hjalmar, for the train of events, for the meaning of the whole: the futile sacrifice of the girl. There is an anticipation of the subsequent Freudian theory of parapraxis, the interpretation of "slips" in relation to the individual's past experiences as well as to his desires and the unity of the two. Freud's hypothesis that "all our experiences have a meaning,"[11] translates this traditional dramatic idea into psychological realism, out of which Ibsen's tragi-comedy, the *Wild Duck,* once again struck the sparks of a dramatic form. When symbolism frees itself from its psychological determination it reifies itself into a self-contained entity, the symbol then becoming symbolistic as in Ibsen's late works, such as *John Gabriel Borkman,* where the clerk, Foldal, is run over by the so-called younger generation, by Youth itself. The contradiction between Ibsen's consistent symbolism and his conservative realism is responsible for the inadequacy of the last plays. Yet it also serves as catalyst for the expressionistic Strindberg. His symbols break free of the empirical individual and are woven into a tapestry in which everything is symbolic, and therefore nothing is symbolic, since anything can signify anything. The drama need only reflect on the inevitable comedy of such self-annulling pansymbolism, grasp it and put it to use, in order for the immanent dialectic of its form to arrive at Beckett's absurdity. Non-significance becomes the only significance. The mortal anxiety of the *dramatis personae,* if not of the parodied drama itself, is the burlesqued fear of meaning something:

> *Hamm.* We're not beginning to . . . to . . . mean something?
> *Clov.* Mean something! You and I, mean something! (*Brief laugh.*) Ah that's a good one! (32–33)

With the disappearance of this possibility, long since suppressed by the overwhelming power of an apparatus in which individuals are exchangeable or superfluous, the meaning of language also vanishes. Hamm, irritated by the bumbling signs of life in his parents' conversation in the trashcans, grows nervous: "Will this never finish?" and

[11] Sigmund Freud, *Gesammelte Werke,* Vol. XI (London, 1940), 33.

he asks: "What's she blathering about? What is there left to blather about?" (23) [12] The play never betrays this insight. At its root is a taboo on language, which it articulates through its very structure. In so doing, it does not shirk the aporia of Expressionist drama: the fact that even where language tends to reduce itself to pure sound, it can never entirely divest itself of its semantic element and become purely mimetic[13] or gestural, just as painting which, however much it has emancipated itself from objective representation, is never entirely free of a certain resemblance to the object-world. Once they have been definitely separated from meaning, mimetic values succumb to the arbitrary and contingent, finally forming a second convention. The manner in which *Endgame* copes with this problem distinguishes it from *Finnegan's Wake*. Instead of striving to liquidate the discursive element of language through pure sound, Beckett transforms it into an instrument of its own absurdity, patterned after the ritual of the clown, whose babble becomes nonsense through its pretense at being meaningful. The objective disintegration of language, which transforms the discourse of men in their own mouths into a stereotyped and false jargon of self-estrangement, penetrates the aesthetic arcanum; the second tongue of the mute, an agglomeration of insulting phrases, specious logic, galvanized words like brand names, the raucous echo of the advertising world, is changed into the language of poetry, which negates language.[14] In this respect, Beckett's drama resembles those of Ionesco. If one of Beckett's later plays is built around the image of the tape-recorder, the language of *Endgame* suggests that abominable social "game" in which the nonsense spoken during a party is secretly recorded in order to humiliate the guests by playing it over again. The shock that ensues, scarcely masked by embarrassed giggles, is developed to its bitter end by Beckett. Just as the reader of Kafka is often struck by Kafkaesque scenes in reality, the audience infected with Beckett is liable to suddenly overhear itself speaking like a character in *Endgame*. The moviegoer who has just left the theater is familiar with the experience of observing the events on the street as though they were a continuation of the film's planned contingency. Between the clichés of ordinary language which comprise the montage of *Endgame*, there gapes a hole. When one of the main characters, with the routine gesture of the person hardened to the inescapable boredom of existence, asks "What in God's name could there be on the horizon?" (31), the linguistic shrug becomes apocalyptic, above

[12] The last sentence is omitted in the English translation (Translator's note).

[13] Cf. Th. W. Adorno, "Voraussetzungen," in *Noten zur Literatur III* (Frankfurt am Main, 1967), und *Dialektik der Aufklärung*, p. 37ff.

[14] Cf. Th. W. Adorno, *Dissonanzen*, 2nd edition (Göttingen, 1958), pp. 34, 44.

all by virtue of its utter familiarity. The slick, aggressive gesture of sound commonsense—"What in God's name could there be?"—is compelled into admitting its own nihilism. Later on, Hamm, the master, commands Clov, the self-declared servant, to perform a circus trick, the futile task of pushing the chair back and forth, of "getting the gaff." This is followed by a short dialogue:

> *Clov.* Do this, do that, and I do it. I never refuse. Why?
> *Hamm.* You're not able to.
> *Clov.* Soon I won't do it any more.
> *Hamm.* You won't be able to any more. (*Exit Clov.*) Ah the creatures, the creatures, everything has to be explained to them. (43)

The fact that "everything has to be explained to them," is incessantly drummed into millions of underlings by their superiors every day. The nonsense which is supposed to justify this in the play—Hamm's explanation refutes his own command—not only serves to expose the absurdity of the cliché, which is otherwise concealed by routine, but also to express the fraudulency of dialogue, the fact that the two interlocutors, hopelessly separated, come no closer through conversing than do the two old cripples in the garbage cans. Communication, the universal law of the cliché, proclaims the end of communication. The absurdity of all speech is not set in an unmediated fashion against realism but rather developed out of it. Through its syntactic form, its logic, its inferences and its traditional concepts, communicative speech necessarily posits the law of sufficient cause. This claim, however, can hardly be met any longer; in conversation with each other, people are motivated partly by their psychology, by the prelogical unconscious, partly by aims of self-preservation, which as such diverge from that objectivity reflected in the logical forms. Today, in any case, that can be demonstrated to them with the tape-recorder. In the sense both of Freud and of Pareto, the *ratio* of verbal communication remains also rationalization. *Ratio* itself, however, arose in the interest of self-preservation, and hence, its inexorable rationalization exposes its own irrationality. The contradiction between the rational facade and the ineluctably irrational is itself already the Absurd. Beckett has only to mark it, to employ it as a principle of selection, in order for realism, divested of all semblance of rational stringency, to pronounce judgment upon itself.

Even the syntax of the question-and-answer form is undermined. It presupposes the open character of what is to be said, something which, as Huxley already has shown, no longer exists. The question already includes the predetermined answer, and this condemns the game of question-and-answer to be an empty delusion, the vain attempt to veil the unfreedom of informative language with the linguistic gesture of freedom. Beckett destroys these masks, including that of philosophy. The pose that invokes Nothingness in order to call everything "radically" into question, employs a pathos stolen from theology in order to hinder in advance those "frightful" Consequences which it so exploits, and employs its questioning stance in order to infiltrate the answer with precisely the meaning that its question ostensibly doubts. It was no accident that such "destructive" spirits were able to defame and devastate the truly destructive, critical intellect during the fascist and pre-fascist eras. Beckett, however, deciphers the lie of the question-mark: the question has become rhetorical. If the inferno of Existentialist philosophy resembled the middle of a tunnel, from where the light at the other end is already visible once again, Beckett's dialogue tears up the rails of dialogue; the train no longer reaches the point where it begins to get light. Wedekind's old technique of misunderstandings is totalized. The course of the dialogue itself approaches the contingency-principle of the literary process of production. It is as if the progression of the dialogue was based not on the law of statement and response, or even on their psychological interrelations, but rather on a certain kind of patient listening-to-the-end, related to that of music which has emancipated itself from preexisting types. The drama listens attentively to each word, as though wondering what will come next. This initial, involuntary questioning fully reveals the absurdity of its contents. This, too, has its infantile model in the people who wait in the zoo to see what the crocodile or chimpanzee will do next.

In its decomposed state, language polarizes. It becomes both Basic English, or French or German, single words, archaically sputtered commands in the jargon of universal disrespect, the familiarity of irreconcilable partners, and the sum of its empty forms, of a grammar which has abandoned all relation to its content, and thus has lost its synthetic function. The interjections are joined by exercise-phrases, God knows to what end. This, too, Beckett makes public: one of the rules of *Endgame* is that the asocial partners, and with them, the audience, are constantly exposing their own game. Hamm feels himself to be an artist. He has chosen Nero's *qualis artifex pereo* as the maxim of his life. But his projected stories run astrand on their syntax:

> *Hamm*. Where was I? (*Pause*. *Gloomily*.) It's finished, we're finished. (*Pause*.) Nearly finished.[15] (50)

[15] Cf. the French text, where the paradigm is clearer: "C'est cassé nous sommes cassés . . . Ça va casser." *Fin de Partie* (Paris, 1957), p. 70 [Translator's note].

Between the paradims, logic has its playground. Hamm and Clov converse in their authoritarian, mutually cutting fashion:

Hamm. Open the window.
Clov. What for?
Hamm. I want to hear the sea.
Clov. You wouldn't hear it.
Hamm. Even if you opened the window?
Clov. No.
Hamm. Then it's not worthwhile opening it?
Clov. No.
Hamm (*violently*). Then open it! (*Clov gets up on the ladder, opens the window. Pause.*) Have you opened it?
Clov. Yes. (64–65)

In Hamm's last "then," one is tempted to seek the key of the drama. Because it is not worthwhile opening the window, since Hamm cannot hear the sea—perhaps it has dried up, perhaps it no longer moves—he insists that Clov open it. The senselessness of an action becomes the reason for doing it, subsequent legitimation of Fichte's free action for its own sake. This is how contemporary actions appear, and one tends to suspect that it was never very different. The logical figure of the absurd, which stringently presents the contradiction of stringency, negates the coherence of meaning, apparently guaranteed by logic, in order to convict the latter of its immanent absurdity: its treatment of the nonidentical, of subject, predicate and copula, as though it were identical, capable of being assimilated to logical forms. It is not as a world-view that the absurd replaces the rational, but as its innermost truth.

The prestabilized harmony of despair governs the relation between the formal aspects of *Endgame* and its residual contents. The shrivelled ensemble counts only four heads. Two of them are excessively red, as though their vitality were a skin disease, whereas the two old persons, as though by way of compensation, are excessively white, like potatoes sprouting in the cellar. None of them has a properly functioning body any longer; the two parents consist only of torsos, having lost their legs not in the catastrophe itself but apparently in a private tandem accident in the Ardennes, "on the road to Sedan," (16), where in the First World War one army did its best to destroy the other—just in case anyone might have imagined that things had changed much since then. Even the memory of their particular misfortune becomes enviable in face of the indeterminacy of the general cataclysm—they laugh while remembering. In distinction to the fathers and sons of Expressionism, all of *Endgame*'s characters have proper names, yet all four are monosyllabic, four-letter words, like obscenities. The practical and familiar abbreviations that are popular in Anglo-Saxon countries are unmasked as the torsos of names. Nell, the aged mother's name, is the only one which is somewhat customary, if obsolete; Dickens uses it for the touching child in *The Old Curiosity Shop*. The three others are invented, as though for billboards. The old man is called Nagg, associated with nagging, and perhaps also with the German, *nagen,* to gnaw, the stuff of their married life. They discuss whether or not the sawdust in their trashcans has been changed, but there is no more sawdust, only sand. Nagg notes that it once was sawdust, and Nell replies irritably, "once" (17), like a wife maliciously mimicking the routinely repeated clichés of her husband. However trivial the argument over sawdust or sand, the difference is decisive to the residual plot, the transition from bare minimum to nothing. Baudelaire's capacity to say the most extreme things with the most extreme discretion, noted by Walter Benjamin,[16] is shared by Beckett. The all too easy consolation that things could be worse becomes a grim verdict. In the realm between life and death, in which not even suffering is possible any longer, the difference between sawdust and sand becomes all-important; sawdust, miserable by-product of the world of things becomes a luxury and its absence signifies the intensification of the life-long death-sentence. The fact that the two live in trashcans—a similar motif can be found in Tennessee Williams' *Camino Real,* although the two plays were surely written independently of each other—results from the technique of taking ordinary phrases literally, a device exploited by Kafka as well.[17] "Nowadays old people are treated like trash"—and that is precisely what happens. *Endgame* is true gerontology. The elderly are superfluous in terms of the socially useful work that they no longer perform; hence, they are thrown away. This truth is snatched from the obfuscation of scientistic jargon in the welfare state which proclaims precisely that which it negates. *Endgame* trains for the time when everyone can expect to find his parents under the lid of the next large trashcan. The natural affinities of the living have become organic waste. The National Socialists irrevocably overthrew the taboo of old age. Beckett's trashcans are emblems of a culture reconstructed in the shadow of Auschwitz. Yet the subplot goes farther than too far: it goes to the end of the aged couple. They are denied their pap, babyfood, which is replaced by

[16] Walter Benjamin, *Schriften I* (Frankfurt am Main 1955), p. 457. [Benjamin (1892–1940), a German critic and essayist, concerned himself, like Adorno, with contemporary cultural phenomena—ED.]

[17] Cf. Th. W. Adorno, "Notes on Kafka," *Prisms,* p. 255 (translator's note).

a biscuit that their toothless mouths can no longer chew; they strangle because the Last Man is too delicate to permit the Next-to-the-Last to survive. This is related to the main plot inasmuch as the demise of the elderly couple anticipates that final exit, the possibility of which constitutes the chief element of dramatic suspense. *Hamlet* is varied: to croak or not to croak, that is the question.

The name of Shakespeare's hero is grimly abbreviated by that of Beckett's chief protagonist, an abbreviation which befits the relation of the last, liquidated dramatic subject to the first. The name also suggests a son of Noah, and thus recalls the great flood: the patriarch of the blacks replaces in a Freudian negation the white master-race. And finally, the "ham" actor. Beckett's Hamm, master of the keys and at the same time impotent, plays the role he no longer is as though he had studied recent sociological literature, which defines the *zoon politikon* as a role. Personality once designated the individual who was adept at putting on airs, at producing himself, just as hapless Hamm does in *Endgame*. Personality itself may, in its origins, have been a role: that of nature pretending to be supernatural. The change of situations in the play occasions an alteration in Hamm's roles: a stage-direction drastically demands that he speak with the "voice of a rational being" (33); in his circuitous narrative he poses with a "narrative tone." The recollection of the irrevocable past becomes a swindle. The process of decomposition condemns in retrospect the continuity of life as a fiction, yet without this continuity there would have been no life. The difference in intonation between narration and mere speech holds court over the principle of identity. Both tones alternate in Hamm's long soliloquy, a kind of inserted aria without music. He stops at the breaks with the artificial pauses of the accomplished actor, in the grand style. If Existentialist philosophy advocated that human beings, no longer capable of being anything else, should at least be themselves, *Endgame* postulates the antithesis to this norm by revealing this very Self to be something else, the aping of something nonexistent. Hamm's hypocrisy brings to light the lie spoken every time the word "I" is pronounced with the intention of arrogating that substantiality which in fact is the very opposite of all that is meant by the notion "I." What alone remains as the quintessence of transience is its ideology. All that survives of the truth-content of the subject, thinking, is its empty gesture. The two main characters act as though they were reflecting upon something, without really reflecting:

> *Hamm*. The whole thing is comical, I grant you that. What about having a good guffaw the two of us together?

Clov (after reflection). I couldn't guffaw again today.
Hamm (after reflection). Nor I. (60)

Hamm's opposite number is what his name indicates: the doubly damaged clown; his last letter has been amputated. Related are also an obsolete expression for the devil's "cloven" hoof, and the more modern, "glove." He is his master's devil and threatens him with the worst he has at his command: leaving him; at the same time, he is Hamm's glove, through which Hamm touches the world of things, a world he can no longer reach directly. Such associations compose not merely the figure of Clov, but its relations to the others. The cover of the old piano edition of Stravinsky's "Ragtime for Eleven Instruments," one of the most important compositions of his surrealist period, displayed a Picasso drawing, probably inspired by the title, "rag," which depicted two ragged figures, forefathers of the vagabonds, Vladimir and Estragon, who await Mr. Godot. The virtuoso engraving consists of a single line. *Endgame*'s double sketch is drawn in this spirit, as are the lame repetitions which permeate Beckett's work as a whole. History is anulled in them. Compulsive repetition is drawn from the regressive behavior of the prisoner who tries over and over again. Not the least of Beckett's affinities to the most recent tendencies in modern music is the manner in which he, the occidental, combines features from Stravinsky's radical past, the frightening stasis of disintegrating continuity, with the most advanced expressive and constructive techniques of the Schoenberg school. The outlines of Hamm and Clov are also those of a single line; they are denied the individuation of clear-cut, disparate monads. They cannot live without each other. Hamm's power over Clov seems to rest on the fact that he alone knows how to open the larder, just as only one director knows the combination of the firm's safe. He would be willing to tell him the secret if Clov would swear "to finish" him—or "us." In an exchange highly characteristic for the texture of the play, Clov replies: "I couldn't finish you," and as though the drama ridiculed all rational pretenses of man, Hamm says: "Then you won't finish me." (37) He must rely on Clov because Clov alone can perform the tasks which keep both alive. This is of dubious value, however, since both are plagued by the fear of the Flying Dutchman: not to be able to die. The fragment of hope, which means everything, is that perhaps this might change. This movement, or its absence, constitutes the action of the play. Of course, it never becomes more explicit than the reiterated leitmotif, "something is taking its course" (13, 32), as abstract as the pure form of time. The Hegelian dialectic of master and servant, the importance of which has already been discussed by Günther Anders in his essay on *Godot,* is not so much presented, in its relation to traditional aesthetic mores, as it is ridiculed. The servant is no longer capable of seizing the reins and abolishing domination. A mutilated Clov no longer has the energy required for such emancipation, and spontaneous action is already out of date according to the historical sun-dial of the drama. There is nothing left for Clov to do except to emigrate to a world which no longer exists for the dearly departed, and thus to have the small chance of dying on the way. Even the right to die is no longer certain for him. He does, it is true, make the decision to leave, and he appears as though ready to depart: "Panama hat, tweed coat, rain coat over his arm, umbrella, bag" (82)—as though in a musical finale. But one does not see him actually exit: instead, he remains "impassive and motionless, his eyes fixed on Hamm, till the end" (82). It is an allegory whose intentionality has run out of steam. Apart from the differences which could either be decisive or entirely irrelevant, it is identical with the beginning. Neither spectator nor philosopher could say with any assurance whether or not the whole thing will begin again from the beginning. Dialectics has run down.

The drama's plot is composed musically upon two themes, like a double-fugue. The first theme is that everything ought to end, the inconspicuous vestige of Schopenhauer's denial of the Will to Life. It is introduced by Hamm; persons who are no longer persons become the instruments of their situation, as though they had to play chamber music. "Of all of Beckett's bizarre instruments, it is Hamm, sitting throughout *Endgame,* blind and motionless in his wheelchair, who has the greatest variety of tones, the most surprising sound." [18] Hamm's nonidentity with himself motivates the development. Whereas he seeks the end of an interminable existence of agony, he is as concerned about his life as a man in his ominiously "best years." The most trivial paraphernalia of health have an exaggerated importance for him. He does not fear death, but only the chance that it might miscarry, an echo of Kafka's *Hunter Gracchus.*[19] No less important to him than his own basic needs is that Clov, ordered to look outside, not see a sail or a wisp of smoke, that no rats or insects are left, from which the catastrophe could develop all over again; that there be no surviving child, the embodiment of hope, for which he searches as did Herod, the butcher, for the *agnus dei.* Insecticide, which from its very inception pointed towards the death camps, becomes the end-product of the domination of nature, putting the finishing touches on

[18] Marie Luise von Kaschnitz, "Vortrag über Lucky," Frankfurt University.
[19] Cf. Th. W. Adorno, *Prisms,* p. 260.

its own annihilation. All that remains of life is the determination that nothing living will be allowed to survive. Everything existing shall be made the equal of a life which is itself death, abstract domination. The second theme is assigned to Clov, the servant. According to a highly obscure story, he came to Hamm seeking aid; all the same, he greatly resembles the son of the raging, impotent patriarch. To reject the domination of the powerless is perhaps the most difficult task of all: everything trivial and obsolete irresistibly opposes emancipation. These two themes are counterpointed through the fact that Hamm's death-will is identical with the principle of his life, whereas Clov's life-will seems destined to bring about the death of both. Hamm says: "Outside of here, it's death" (9). The antithesis of the heroes is not fixed, however; their impulses mingle. It is Clov who first speaks of the end. The progression is patterned on the scheme of the end-game in chess, a typical situation, governed by a set of norms, separated from the middle-game and its combinations by a caesura; the latter are also absent from the play, which tacitly suspends intrigue and plot. Only artistic blunders or accidents, such as the remark that living things are still growing somewhere, could provide surprises—not true ingenuity. The field is virtually empty and what came before can only be deciphered with difficulty from the poses of the few remaining figures. Hamm is the monarch around whom everything turns and who himself can accomplish nothing. The disproportion between chess as a hobby and the enormous effort that it entails is brought on stage in the form of the athletic gesticulations of the characters and the contrast they make with the rubber-weight of their actual accomplishments. Whether the game ends with a stalemate or an eternal check, or whether Clov wins, is left ambiguous, as though certainty would be too meaningful; moreover, it is not terribly important, since everything would come to rest in a stalemate no less than in mate itself. Otherwise, it is only the fleeting image of the small boy (78), which stands out, fragile reminiscence of Fortinbras or of the child-king. It could even be Clov's own, deserted child. But the half-light that shines into the room from this image is as feeble as the helplessly helping arms which stretch from the window at the end of Kafka's *Trial*.

The final history of the subject becomes thematic in an intermezzo which can only afford its symbolism because it never overlooks its own fragility and that of its meaning. The hybris of idealism, which enthroned man as the creator in the center of the creation, has barricaded itself in this "bare interior," like a tyrant in his last days: with a microscopically reduced imagination, he repeats what man once conceived as his destiny, an ideal ruined for him no less by the development of society than by that of modern cosmology, and yet from which he cannot break away. Clov is his male nurse. Hamm lets him push him in his wheelchair into the middle of that interior, which is all that is left of the world and which at the same time is the interior of his own subjectivity:

Hamm. Take me for a little turn. (*Clov goes behind the chair and pushes it forward.*) Not too fast! (*Clov pushes chair.*) Right round the world! (*Clov pushes chair.*) Hug the walls, then back to the center again. (*Clov pushes chair.*) I was right in the center, wasn't I? (25)

The loss of center which this parodies, because that center itself was already a lie, becomes the miserable object of nagging, impotent pedantry:

Clov. We haven't done the round.
Hamm. Back to my place! (*Clov pushes chair back to center.*) Is that my place?
Clov. Yes, that's your place.
Hamm. Am I right in the center?
Clov. I'll measure it.
Hamm. More or less! More or less!
Clov (*moving chair slightly*). There!
Hamm. I'm more or less in the center?
Clov. I'd say so.
Hamm. You'd say so! Put me right in the center!
Clov. I'll go and get the tape.
Hamm. Roughly! Roughly! (*Clov moves chair slightly.*) Bang in the center! (26–27)

Yet what is avenged in the idiotic ritual is nothing that the subject previously did. Subjectivity itself is the guilt, the fact that one exists at all. The original sin is heretically fused to the creation. Being, which Existentialist philosophy proclaimed the meaning of being, becomes its antithesis. The reflex-movements of anything living provokes a panic which not only strives insatiably to dominate nature but moreover attacks life itself, which it confuses with the catastrophe that this life has become:

Hamm. All those I might have helped. (*Pause.*) Helped! (*Pause.*) Saved. (*Pause.*) Saved! (*Pause.*) The place was crawling with them! (*Pause. Violently.*) Use your head, can't you, use your head, you're on earth, there's no cure for that! (68)

He draws the conclusion: "The end is in the beginning and yet you go on." (69) The autonomous moral law turns antinomially around, pure domination over nature becomes the essence it always concealed: the duty to exterminate.

> *Hamm.* More complications! (*Clov gets down.*) Not an underplot, I trust. (*Clov moves ladder nearer window, gets up on it, turns telescope on the without.*)
> *Clov* (*dismayed*). Looks like a small boy!
> *Hamm* (*sarcastic*). A small . . . boy!
> *Clov.* I'll go and see. (*He gets down, drops the telescope, goes towards door, turns.*) I'll get the gaff. (78)

The idealism, from which this notion of total duty arose, is judged by a question that Clov, the frustrated rebel, puts to his frustrated master:

> *Clov.* Any particular sector you fancy? Or merely the whole thing? (73)

This sounds like the test of Benjamin's insight that a single cell of reality, subjected to the most minute scrutiny, would reveal all the rest of reality. The totality, pure postulation of the subject, is Nothing. No proposition sounds more absurd than this most rational one, which reduces Everything to Merely, and thus exposes the illusion of an anthropocentrically dominated world. Yet as rational as this greatest of absurdities may be, the absurd aspect of Beckett's play cannot be discussed away simply because it was appropriated by ready apologists and zealous labellers. Reason, which has become totally instrumental, deprived of all self-reflection and of reflection upon that which it, in the course of its development, disqualified, must interrogate the meaning which it itself eliminated. In the stage at which this question has become obligatory, there remains no response except that of Nothingness, which reason in its pure form already is. The historical inexorability of this absurdity endows it with a semblance of ontology: this is the hallucination of history itself. Beckett's drama explodes it. The immanent contradiction of the Absurd, of the nonsense in which reason terminates, inaugurates emphatically the possibility of a truth which cannot even be conceived any longer. It undermines the absolute pretension of that which happens to exist. Negative ontology is the negation of ontology: History alone has engendered what the mythical power of the timeless has appropriated. The historical fibre of situation and language in Beckett does not concretize, *more philosophico,* something unhistorical—precisely this tendency of Existentialist drama is as anti-aesthetic as it is philosophically retarded. Beckett's once-and-for-all is, on the contrary, the unending catastrophe; the fact "that the earth is extinguished, though I never saw it lit" (81) justifies Clov's answer to Hamm's question:

"Do you not think this has gone on long enough?"—"I've always thought so" (45). Prehistory continues, the fantasm of eternity is only its curse. After Clov has reported back to his crippled master what he has seen of the earth, which Hamm had ordered him to observe, the latter confides in him:

Clov (*absorbed*). Mmm.
Hamm. Do you know what it is?
Clov (*as before*). Mmm.
Hamm. I was never there. (74)

The earth was never walked upon; the subject is not yet one.

Determinate negation is dramatized through consistent inversion. The two social partners modify their insight that there is no more nature with the bourgeois qualification, "you exaggerate" (11). Sobriety is the tried and tested means of sabotaging thought. It gives rise to the melancholy reflection:

Clov (*sadly*). No one that ever lived thought so crooked as we. (11)

Whenever they come closest to the truth, they sense, in a double comedy, their consciousness to be false; this is how a situation which has become inaccessible to reflection reflects itself. Yet the play is woven into a whole by means of this technique of inversion. It transfigures the empirical world into what the late Strindberg and the Expressionists had already named it. "The whole place stinks of corpses . . . The whole universe." (46) Hamm, who thereupon condemns the universe—"To hell with the universe" (46)—is no less the great-grandson of Fichte, scorning the world as mere raw material and product, than he is the person who knows no other hope than that of the cosmic night which he supplicates with poetic citations. The world as an absolute becomes the inferno: nothing exists outside of it. "Beyond is the . . . other hell." (26) Beckett allows an involuted, secular metaphysics to shine through, with Brechtian commentary:

Clov. Do you believe in the life to come?
Hamm. Mine was always that. (*Exit Clov.*) Got him that time! (49)

Benjamin's notion of dialectics at a standstill finds a home in Hamm's conception:

Hamm. It will be the end and there I'll be, wondering what can have brought it on and wondering what can have . . . (*he hesitates*) . . . why it was so long coming. (*Pause.*) There I'll be, in the old refuge, alone against the silence and . . . (*he hesitates*) . . . the stillness. If I can hold my peace, and sit quiet, it will be all over, with sound, and motion, all over and done with. (69)

That stillness is the order that Clov claims to love and that he defines as the purpose of his activity:

Clov. A world where all would be silent and still and each thing in its last place, under the last dust. (57)

The Old Testament, "dust thou shall become," is translated into: filth. The excretions become the substance of a life that is death. But the imageless image of death is one of indifference. In it vanishes the distinction between absolute domination, the hell in which time in its totality is confined in a space, in which there is absolutely no more change, and the messianic state in which everything would be in its proper place. The final absurdity is that the repose of nothingness and that of reconciliation cannot be distinguished. Hope crawls out of a world in which it is no better safeguarded than pap and candy, back to where it started: to death. This alone gives the play its sole consolation, that of the stoics:

Clov. There are so many terrible things.
Hamm. No, no, there are not so many now. (44)

Consciousness makes ready to look its own end in the face as though it sought to survive it, just as Beckett's two figures seek to outlive the end of their world. Proust, to whom Beckett devoted an essay in his youth, is said to have sought to record his own struggle with death in the form of notes, which were then to have been inserted into the description of Bergotte's death. *Endgame* fulfills this intention like the executor of a testament.

Chronology of Important Dates

[Note: Listed in the language in which they were first written, Beckett's dramatic works are dated by first performance, his non-dramatic works by first publication.]

	Beckett	*The Age*
1906	April 13: Born at Foxrock, near Dublin	Death of Cezanne; Picasso begins "Les Desmoiselles d'Avignon"
1911		Stravinsky, "Rites of Spring"
1912		Schoenberg, "Pierrot Lunaire"; Kafka, "The Metamorphosis"
1913		Proust, *Swann's Way*; Husserl, *Ideas: General Introduction to Pure Phenomenology*
1917		First jazz recording by the Original Dixieland "Jass" Band
1919		Wiene, "Cabinet of Dr. Caligari"
1921		Pirandello, *Six Characters in Search of an Author*
1922		Eliot, "Wasteland"; Joyce, *Ulysses*; Joyce begins *Finnegan's Wake*
1927		Buster Keaton stars in "The General"
1930	"Whoroscope," poem on Descartes	

1931	*Proust*	
1938	*Murphy*	Artaud, *The Theatre and its Double*; Sartre, *Nausea*; Bram van Velde, Beckett's favorite painter, shown in Peggy Guggenheim's London gallery
1943		Peggy Guggenheim begins showing Abstract Expressionists and Action painters in New York; Sartre, *Being and Nothingness, No Exit*
1947		Genet, *The Maids*
1951	*Molloy, Malone Meurt*	
1952		Ionesco, *The Chairs*
1953	*En Attendant Godot,* Theatre Babylone, Paris; *Watt, L'Innomable*	
1955	*Waiting for Godot,* Arts Theatre, London; *Nouvelles et Textes pour Rien*	Robbe-Grillet, *Le Voyeur*
1957	*All That Fall,* BBC; *Fin de Partie,* Royal Court Theatre, London	
1958	*Krapp's Last Tape* and *Endgame,* Royal Court Theatre, London	
1959	*Embers,* BBC	
1960		Godard, *Breathless*; Pinter, *The Caretaker*
1961	*Happy Days,* Cherry Lane Theatre, New York; *Comment C'est*	
1962	*Words and Music,* BBC	
1963	*Cascando,* RTF, Paris	
1964	*Play,* Cherry Lane; *Film* produced in New York, starring Buster Keaton	
1966	*Eh Joe,* BBC television	

Notes on the Editor and Contributors

BELL GALE CHEVIGNY, editor of this volume, received her Ph.D. at Yale and teaches literature at Sarah Lawrence College. Her publications include an essay on Gerard Manley Hopkins, book reviews on contemporary literature, and articles on political subjects.

THEODOR W. ADORNO is a philosopher, composer, sociologist and literary critic. His books in German include works on Kierkegaard, Hegel, Husserl and the phenomenologists, and a theory of negative dialectic; and studies of Alban Berg (his teacher), Mahler, Wagner, a sociology of music, and a philosophy of the new music of Schoenberg and Stravinsky. On the strength of the last work, he became Thomas Mann's "musical adviser" for the novel *Doctor Faustus*. Having left Germany in 1933, he collaborated at the Institute for Social Research in New York on *The Authoritarian Personality* (1950). Other works in English include his essay-collection *Prisms* (Neville Spearman, 1967) and a volume of essays to be brought out in 1970 by Farrar, Strauss and Giroux.

ROSS CHAMBERS teaches French at the University of New South Wales, Sydney. He is the author of *Gérard de Nerval et la poétique du voyage* and of articles on nineteenth- and twentieth-century French literature.

RUBY COHN, Professor of English and Comparative Literature at San Francisco State College, is author of *Samuel Beckett: The Comic Gamut* (1962), *Currents in Modern Drama,* and *Edward Albee*. She has also edited the special Beckett issue of *Perspective* (1959) and many books, including *Casebook on Waiting for Godot* (1967).

ANTONY EASTHOPE, educated at Cambridge University, has taught English at Brown University and at the University of Warwick, Coventry. He is currently working on a book on tragedy.

MARTIN ESSLIN is Head of the Radio Drama Department of the British Broadcasting Corporation, London. He is author of *Brecht* (1959) and *The Theatre of the Absurd* (1961), and he edited *Samuel Beckett: A Collection of Critical Essays.*

RICHARD M. GOLDMAN teaches English at the State University of New York at Albany. His special interests are in Shakespeare and modern drama.

Hugh Kenner, Professor of English at the University of California, Santa Barbara, is author of *Samuel Beckett: A Critical Study* (1961), *Flaubert, Joyce and Beckett: The Stoic Comedians* (1962) as well as works on Pound, Joyce, Eliot, and Wyndham Lewis. He edited *T. S. Eliot: A Collection of Critical Essays.*

Alan Schneider, who has a special interest in Beckett, has directed all of Beckett's plays in New York, most of Edward Albee's, and some of Harold Pinter's. He is also a writer and has lectured at Catholic University.

Selected Bibliography

Blau, Herbert, *The Impossible Theatre: A Manifesto*. New York: Macmillan Co., 1964, pp. 240–51. In an impressionistic essay, the co-founder of the Actor's Workshop of San Francisco tells how, in his production of *Endgame*, he interpreted character, speech, gesture, and set-design by means of the central premise that the play telescoped "thousands of years of cultural history."

Eastman, Richard, "The Strategy of Samuel Beckett's *Endgame*," *Modern Drama*, II (May, 1959), 36–44. Useful as an introduction to the play's structural ideas, this study also eloquently insists on the play's humanity in an anti-human context.

Kott, Jan, "King Lear or Endgame," *Shakespeare Our Contemporary*. Garden City, New York: Doubleday & Company Inc., 1964, pp. 87–124. Distinguishing classic tragic form from the modern grotesque, this chapter shows *Lear* anticipating the grotesque and, rather cursorily, *Godot*, *Endgame*, and *Act Without Words* reproducing *Lear* "in its skeleton form."

Lyons, Charles R., "Beckett's *Endgame*: An Anti-Myth of Creation," *Modern Drama*, VII (September, 1964), 204–9. This essay argues briefly that the play's action is the disintegration of consciousness and traces, through imagery, the reversal of the myth of creation, and the return to the void.

Mayoux, Jean-Jacques, "The Theatre of Samuel Beckett," *Perspective*, XI (Autumn, 1959), 142–55. An excellent introduction to Beckett's theatre, its meaning and uses in defining man's fate, its consequences for language, this study also makes illuminating connections to Shakespeare, Strindberg, Ibsen, and Kafka.

Robbe-Grillet, Alain, "Samuel Beckett, or 'Presence' in the Theatre," *For A New Novel*, translated by Richard Howard. New York: Grove Press, Inc., 1965, pp. 111–25. Robbe-Grillet demonstrates how Beckett interprets the fundamental theatrical condition of being " 'on the scene': *there*" in *Godot* and *Endgame*.

Scott, Nathan A., *Samuel Beckett*. London: Bowes & Bowes, 1965. Beckett is located in a survey of literary faiths beginning with Baudelaire. A brief discussion of *Endgame* compares its "Zero" with Dietrich Bonhoeffer's "grace at zero point," and Beckett's stance with that of Camus and Céline.

Sheedy, John J., "The Comic Apocalypse of King Hamm," *Modern Drama,* IX (December, 1966), 310–18. This suggestive study treats the play's simultaneously comic and apocalyptic dimensions, and follows the logic of the action—at once the passion of Jesus and a chess game—by unusually close analysis of the text.

Tynan, Kenneth, "*Krapp's Last Tape* and *Endgame,* by Samuel Beckett, at the Royal Court," *Curtains.* New York: Atheneum, 1961, pp. 225–28. Picking up Beckett's syntactic rhythms, Tynan offers by way of review a skit, *Slamm's Last Knock,* which reduces Beckett's reductive technique almost to absurdity ("A genius. Could you do as much?" "Not as much. But as little.")

Walker, Roy, "Love, Chess, and Death: Samuel Beckett's Double Bill," *Twentieth Century,* CLXIV (December, 1958), 533–44. A loose and lively set of responses to the London productions of *Endgame* and *Krapp's Last Tape,* this is suggestive in its account of the characters' relationships, the play's puns, and its current relevance.

TWENTIETH CENTURY INTERPRETATIONS

MAYNARD MACK, *Series Editor*
Yale University

NOW AVAILABLE
Collections of Critical Essays
ON

ADVENTURES OF HUCKLEBERRY FINN
ALL FOR LOVE
THE AMBASSADORS
ARROWSMITH
AS YOU LIKE IT
BLEAK HOUSE
THE BOOK OF JOB
THE CASTLE
DOCTOR FAUSTUS
DON JUAN
DUBLINERS
THE DUTCHESS OF MALFI
ENDGAME
EURIPIDES' ALCESTIS
THE FALL OF THE HOUSE OF USHER
THE FROGS
GRAY'S ELEGY
THE GREAT GATSBY
GULLIVER'S TRAVELS
HAMLET
HARD TIMES
HENRY IV, PART TWO
HENRY V

(continued on next page)

(continued from previous page)

The Iceman Cometh
Julius Caesar
Keats's Odes
Lord Jim
Much Ado About Nothing
Oedipus Rex
The Old Man and the Sea
Pamela
The Playboy of the Western World
The Portrait of a Lady
A Portrait of the Artist as a Young Man
The Rape of the Lock
The Rime of the Ancient Mariner
Robinson Crusoe
Samson Agonistes
The Scarlet Letter
Sir Gawain and the Green Knight
Songs of Innocence and of Experience
The Sound and the Fury
The Tempest
Tess of the D'Urbervilles
Tom Jones
Twelfth Night
Utopia
Vanity Fair
Walden
The Waste Land
Wuthering Heights